ONE POTATO
TWO POTATO

D0047978

ONE POTATO TWO POTATO

A Cookbook and More!

Janet Reeves

Ragweed Press
Charlottetown
1987

©1987 by Janet Reeves
ISBN 0-920304-70-2

THIRD PRINTING 1990

Illustrations: Brenda Whiteway
Cover photographs: John Sylvester
Book Design: Cape Bear Associates
Typesetting: Braemar Publishing Limited
Printing: Williams & Crue (1982) Ltd.

Ragweed Press
P.O. Box 2023
Charlottetown, Prince Edward Island
Canada   C1A 7N7

Published with the kind assistance of the Department of Communications and the Prince Edward Island Cultural Product Development Fund.

Canadian Cataloguing in Publication Data

Reeves, Janet, 1942–
   One potato, two potato

Includes index.
ISBN 0-920304-70-2

1. Cookery (Potatoes). I. Title

TX803.P8R44 1987   641.6'521   C87-093694-8

We praise all the flowers that we fancy
Sip the nectar of fruit ere they're peeled,
Ignoring the common old tater
When, in fact, he's King of the Field.
Let us show the old boy we esteem him,
Sort of dig him up out of the mud;
Let us show him he shares our affections
And crown him with glory—King Spud.
                                    —Irish Potato Marketing Company

Contents

Acknowledgements

Special thanks go to Dr. O.T. Page, Director of Research (1972–1985), International Potato Centre, Lima, Peru; Dr. Samuel Asiedu, Plant Industry Services, P.E.I. Department of Agriculture; Tom and Meredith Hughes, Potato Museum, Washington, D.C.; Irish Potato Marketing Company, Dublin, Ireland; The Potato Board, Denver, Colorado; the P.E.I. Departments of Agriculture and Fisheries, Charlottetown; the P.E.I. Egg Commodity Marketing Board, Charlottetown; the P.E.I. Potato Marketing Board, Charlottetown; Agriculture Canada, Ottawa; Centro Internacional de La Papa (International Potato Centre or CIP), Lima, Peru; Las Damas Del CIP (CIP Women's Club), Lima, Peru; Margaret Weeks and Gloria Wood, home economists with the P.E.I. Department of Agriculture; Harry Fraser, *Fraser's Newsletter;* La Société Saint-Thomas D'Aquin, Summerside, P.E.I.; John Sylvester and Brenda Whiteway, Charlottetown; Ann Thurlow, Charlottetown, for giving the book its title; Cathy Matthews, Valerie Stewart, Lee Fleming, Mary Lou Brinklow, Susan Wright and Lynn Henry for all their help with proofreading, paste-up and indexing; my publisher Libby Oughton and editor Laurie Brinklow, Ragweed Press, Charlottetown; Linkletter Farms Limited, who supplied the potatoes for recipe-testing—not to mention their boundless enthusiasm; Brenda Rogers, without whose help I could not have completed this mammoth undertaking; my husband Allison and son Mark who ate potatoes three meals a day for several weeks without complaint (and never gained an ounce); and all those who contributed anecdotes and recipes as well as much-needed encouragement and support.

Introduction

This book is an affectionate chronicle of the potato. It tells the story of the potato from its earliest struggle for survival to the attaining of its rightful crown—the World's Number One Vegetable, King Spud.

This rise in fame follows a four-century crusade rife with ignorance, superstition and fear. Today the potato is a part of our way of life—the average person in North America is said to eat one hundred pounds of potatoes a year—yet not long ago people would starve rather than eat one.

In the potato we find a versatile food that is both nutritious and economical. It is easy to prepare as a side vegetable or in a variety of taste-tempting dishes. No other vegetable is served as often or combines as well with other foods as the potato.

One Potato, Two Potato (A Cookbook and More!) is a fascinating record of the potato's pilgrimage. This book includes historical and nutritional facts, illustrations, numerous pieces of trivia and helpful hints, as well as nearly three hundred palate-pleasing recipes dedicated to good food from many kitchens, past and present. The recipes included keep to the basic simplicity and naturalness of our pioneer cooks, yet are adapted for use in today's modern kitchens. You will find new ideas for family meals and festive entertaining, with foods ranging from country classica to international gourmet specialties.

Potatoes form the main ingredient of many dishes, while other recipes, such as the baked products, have been modified to benefit from the inclusion of potatoes. The resulting improvement in texture—while at the same time keeping quality, moistness and flavour—justifies the little extra work involved in using potatoes.

The tested recipes in this book are presented in imperial measurements and can be easily reduced or expanded. However, a metric conversion table is included. Ingredients are listed in order of use and all instructions are clearly stated . . . assuring that every recipe will produce perfect results every time.

Few foods can rival the versatile potato. After researching and writing this book, I, for one, will never again take the potato for granted. The "lowly spud" is indeed "King."

9

The History of the Potato

No one knows the exact origin of the potato. Potato researchers and archaeologists believe that some form of potato was cultivated as far back as 500 B.C. We naturally assume the potato has always been with us, yet the first recorded knowledge of potatoes being used as a staple food goes back just over four centuries, to the Spanish invasion of South America. Little did the conquistadores know that when they went looking for gold, they would also find buried treasure in the potato.

The Incas had found the plants growing wild at altitudes too cold for wheat and corn. They cultivated them and developed some nearly frost-proof varieties. Potatoes were an important part of the Inca way of life. They were used for telling time, treatment of illness and injury, divination, fermenting into drinks, as well as for their main food. The Incas worshipped potato deities. They celebrated rituals and offered occasional human sacrifices to appease the gods. When crops failed, noses and lips of some of the natives were mutilated in ceremonies dedicated to the potato gods. Many early Indian pottery designs also combine potato and human forms.

The Peruvian name for the plant is *papa*, meaning tuber. The Quechua language has over a thousand words to describe potatoes. For example, a long flat potato is called *mishipasinghan* (cat's nose). Misshapen, hard-to-prepare potatoes are *lumchipamundana* (potatoes makes young bride weep).

The Incas used potatoes to prepare what was probably the first freeze-dried food. *Chuño* (choon-yo) is still produced in the highlands of Bolivia, Chile and Peru, using the same age-old techniques. The Indians take the newly harvested potatoes and spread them on the ground to freeze overnight. The potatoes thaw in the hot morning sun and, at midday, barefoot men, women and children trample them, squeezing out the excess moisture. The pulp dries in the afternoon sun. This goes on daily for up to three weeks until the potatoes are reduced to a greyish, dry material that resembles small stones. *Chuño* is as hard as wood, very light-weight and will keep for up to four years. Greyish *chuño* (*chuño negro*) is soaked in at least six to eight changes of water to reduce bitterness and then is used in a variety of dishes. White *chuño (chuño tunta* or *moray)* is made by soaking the freeze-dried *chuño* in streams of running water for several days and then re-drying, removing the grey colour.

Today *chuño* can be bought in crushed, whole or powdered forms. The powder is used instead of wheat in baking bread. As the Inca saying goes, "stew without *chuño* is like life without love."

The Incas also sun-dried cooked potatoes to form *papa seca*, an amber-coloured granular material that was used in soup stock. These products, with their excellent keeping qualities, were then stored for use by the Inca armies and as insurance against famine.

The Spanish explorers, among them Gonzalo Jemenez de Quesada, found the potato to their liking and after the conquest of Peru brought back both potatoes and Inca gold. The potato received mixed reaction in Spain, including distrust and fear. At first they were grown in Galicia and only as a garden novelty.

Little was known about the potato, giving reason for the people's initial fear. The potato belongs to the botanical family *Solanaceae*, which includes many poisonous narcotic and hallucinogenic relatives such as *mandrake* and *bella donna* (also called deadly nightshade). Some potatoes contain *solanine,* which causes a skin rash that sixteenth-century Europeans thought was the beginning of leprosy. And any food growing underground was thought to be both unclean and unchristian.

Before long, however, the potato began to gain a reputation for some medicinal benefits. Cut potatoes were applied to warts, sprains and black eyes. In time they were used for rheumatism, scurvy and as a cure for impotence. Some people, though, still felt potatoes were evil, that they caused flatulence and syphilis, among other things. However, when the potato was labelled as a powerful aphrodisiac, it was on its way—black market prices reached unbelievable heights.

Some of the more adventuresome folk began using potatoes as food around the 1570s. In 1573 potatoes were fed to hospital patients. About this time they were also used for feeding livestock and convicts.

From Spain, the use of the potato spread to Italy, where it was believed that one could dispose of an enemy by writing his name on a potato.

Meanwhile, in 1563, Sir John Hawkins is said to have introduced the potato to England. Its cultivation at this time, however, was sadly neglected. In 1586 the potato was reintroduced, probably by way of one of Sir Francis Drake's ships. England was slow to accept the potato, associating it with squalour. Ironically, it was later thought of as a botanical curiosity and a rich man's delicacy.

In 1619 King James I first served potatoes at the royal table. England introduced potatoes to Flanders during the wars against King Louis XIV. Finally, during the Victorian era, the British upper class began to take the potato seriously.

King Charles II made efforts, between 1660 and 1685, to have commoners plant potatoes. In 1664 an English author wrote a book to promote the "lowly spud." Entitled (along with several subtitles) *England's Happiness Increased, of a Sure and Easie Remedy Against All succeeding Dear Years by a Plantation of Roots called Potatoes*, the book most likely was *not* a best seller, but it probably has the distinction of having the longest title.

The potato arrived in Germany in 1588. Here it was considered a lowly food, suitable for livestock, prisoners and common folk. The upper class wanted nothing to do with food associated with the South American Indians that was also grown underground.

In Scotland the clergy found no mention of potatoes in the Bible and banned them because they were "unholy." In Burgundy and Besancon, potatoes were called Indian artichokes and were forbidden, out of fear of leprosy and syphilis.

By the end of the seventeenth century, potatoes had reached Russia, imported from Holland by Peter the Great, and were served at Imperial banquets. The Russian peasants would not eat them and labelled them unclean and unchristian, saying they were "the Devil's apples." A few centuries later, during the Siege of Leningrad, scientists felt potatoes were so important that they burned furniture to keep a sack of precious seed potatoes from freezing. Although near starvation, they refused to eat the small tubers.

In time, the more enlightened people saw the value of the potato and several kings and emperors initiated national programs of potato planting. In 1740 the potato saved the Irish from famine. In 1744 King William of Germany ordered the peasants to plant potatoes. He distributed potatoes free along with instructions on how to plant them. He then sent soldiers to supervise the planting and threatened to cut off the nose of anyone who disobeyed. Twenty years later an official proclamation forced the people of Sweden to grow potatoes. The inhabitants of Kolbery, Germany, however, remained adamant. As late as 1774, they refused to eat the "sexually unclean" potato, despite the fact that they were in a state of famine. Switzerland associated potatoes with scrofula and were also a long time accepting them.

A French chemist, Antoine August Parmentier, probably did more than anyone else to promote the potato. Parmentier, a soldier in the French army during the Seven Years' War, was captured and imprisoned in Hanover, Germany, for three years. While in prison, he and his friends lived almost entirely on potatoes—food the Germans fed to livestock. Upon returning to France, Parmentier found his country in a state of famine, yet still unwilling to eat the food that had saved his life. The French thought that potatoes would weaken the people and ruin the land. Parmentier declared this fear nonsense and wrote a thesis to promote the potato. His work, entitled *Inquiry Into Nourishing Vegetables That At Times of Necessity Could Be Substituted for Ordinary Food*, was published in 1773 and listed potatoes among the vegetables that could help in times of food shortages. History reports that Parmentier went to the birthday party of King Louis XVI and presented him with a bouquet of potato blossoms. The king put a flower in his buttonhole and Queen Marie Antoinette wore potato flowers in her hair. Almost immediately the aristocracy copied them and potato flowers became the fashion. Potato designs appeared on pottery, china and jewellery.

Parmentier then devised a plan to save the country and popularize the potato as a food. He entertained with elaborate banquets, inviting famous people to his home and serving as many as twenty dishes at each meal, all containing potatoes. Next he persuaded the king to give him fifty arpents (about one acre) of barren soil, just outside the city of Les Sablons, near Paris. Parmentier planted potatoes in the sandy soil and, as harvest time approached, stationed guards around the field during the day. At night the guards were taken away. As he expected, the local peasants, curious about something valuable enough to be guarded, began to pilfer the potato patch.

Before long, potatoes were blossoming all over France. Thanks to Parmentier, the potato became one of France's staple foods as well as a status symbol. Parmentier was called the "Potato Messiah" and today the best potato dishes in France have "Parmentier" in their name. After his death, statues were built to honour Parmentier and for some time potatoes were planted each year on his grave.

By 1813, potatoes were being grown extensively in Scotland and were becoming well-known in Holland, Austria, Switzerland, Germany and Italy.

Historians disagree on who brought the first potato to Ireland. Some say Sir Francis Drake, others Sir Walter Raleigh, and still others think they were found in shipwrecks of Spanish sailors along the coast. They do agree, however, that they were there by 1663 and were given a generous welcome.

Ireland adopted the reliable, uncomplicated potato more readily than any of her neighbours. Potatoes grow easily and abundantly in cool, moist areas. Ireland's soil and climate are ideal. Here potatoes quickly became a dietary staple and were accepted as a national food. Ireland's population increased steadily and potatoes became such an important food that they were quickly named "Irish" potatoes to distinguish them from sweet potatoes.

The potato also became a secret weapon. During the seventeenth-century rebellions in Ireland, the English soldiers tried to quell uprisings by burning or trampling the food crops. But the potato was safely underground.

In 1740 a crop failure caused a famine that resulted in the deaths of about one-fifth of the population, but it did not force the Irish to give up on potatoes. One hundred years later, the population had risen to an all-time high of about nine million people.

Ironically, the ideal climate for growing potatoes is also the ideal condition for one of the potato's worst enemies. This was to prove devastating to the people of Ireland. Until the 1840s, late blight was unheard of in Ireland. In 1845 tragedy struck all of Europe in a scourge of late blight. Late blight is a fungus that starts in the leaves of the plant. From there, spores go into the soil to attack the tubers, destroying the plant within a week. Late blight, although still a universal problem for potato growers, can be controlled with fungicides. In the 1840s, however, there were no such controls and the worst disaster since the Black Death of 1348 to 1350 occurred. Late blight spread through the country causing crop failures from 1845 to 1851.

The first two years were the worst as Ireland's crops were a total failure. Unlike the rest of Europe, Ireland depended almost entirely on potatoes for food. They grew grain and raised cattle, but these other products were exported to their absentee landlords in England. Over a million people died of starvation and disease, and hundreds of thousands emigrated to other countries. The actual count of those who died was never determined, as many people also perished at sea. The overcrowded ships came to be known as coffin ships. Today in Ireland you can still see the mounds where people were buried in mass graves.

By the end of the century, steady emigration and fewer births had cut the population of Ireland in half. The majority of the emigrants settled in the United States. Some also came to Canada, along with many English and Scottish settlers, bringing with them the potato.

Others went to Australia; they were the first immigrants to that country who were not convicts.

Potatoes had been brought to North America via Bermuda as early as 1621. There is evidence of potatoes growing in Port Royal, Nova Scotia, as early as 1623. They were not considered an important crop until the Irish immigrants introduced them to New Hampshire in 1719. As late as 1740, North Americans thought potatoes would shorten men's lives.

Immigrants after the "Great Famine" firmly established the potato in North America. Today, in spite of a history telling a distinct lack of enthusiasm, and various famines and disasters, the potato has gained strength. By the end of the nineteenth century, potatoes were considered a superior food. Today they are grown in one hundred and thirty countries and yield more food on less land than any major crop. They are found almost everywhere in the world, except for the lowland tropics and the polar ice regions (although they are even found in parts of Greenland). Potatoes are the fourth largest world crop, surpassed only by wheat, rice and corn.

It is interesting to note that the potato made history in 1979 by being the first produce item to receive a nutrition label. This label gives nutritionists a guide for analyzing other fruits and vegetables. No longer is the potato a "fattening starch" but is recognized as a nutritious, beneficial vegetable that should be included in every well-balanced diet. Children unable to tolerate milk are given potatoes which provide about seventy-five per cent of their nutritional requirements. Potatoes are being seriously considered as a possible answer to world hunger.

Today the riches of the Inca Empire and the glory of the Spanish conquistadores are only recorded memories. Yet the potato lives on . . . the vegetable that conquered the world.

What Is A Potato?

The potato, *Solanum tuberosum*, is a perennial plant cultivated for its edible starchy tubers. Above the ground the potato has an erect stem with alternately arranged, coarse dark-green compound leaves, resembling those of a tomato. (Tomatoes, along with egg plant, peppers and tobacco, are part of the same botanical family.) The flowers range in colours of white, pink, red or bluish-purple, depending on variety. These flowers develop a small green fruit (seed ball), one-half to one inch in diameter, again resembling the tomato's. Each seed ball contains about three hundred yellowish seeds.

Scientists use these seeds, called true potato seed, in developing new varieties of disease-free potato plants. Like its relative, the deadly nightshade, these seed balls and all green parts of the potato plant are poisonous.

Lateral shoots grow from the main stem of the potato down into the ground. Food made in the leaves passes to the end of these shoots causing them to swell and form tubers. The tuber, or edible part of the potato, is not part of the root as is commonly believed, but is formed by this swelling of the underground stems (or rhizones).

The skin of the potato may range in colour from tan and brown to white, red or purple. The flesh is usually white or light yellowish, with a few varieties having a bluish tinge.

The "eyes" on potatoes are, in fact, tiny leaves and external buds, each of which can produce a new shoot or plant. In North America, potatoes are usually planted by "sets" or "seed pieces" which are portions of potatoes that have at least one to three "eyes" in each piece. These sets are planted in trenches at spaces of 12 to 18 inches, depending on variety. They are covered with a few inches of soil. As the plants grow, additional soil is put up around them to protect the developing tubers. Potatoes require a cool growing season. From the time they are planted it takes from 90 to 140 days for potatoes to reach maturity, depending again on variety and location. All seed potatoes should be government-inspected and certified as suitable for planting. The home gardener should not plant potatoes from the supermarket. These

17

potatoes have usually had a sprout inhibitor sprayed on them and thus will not grow. Your local potato grower will be able to provide you with seed potatoes.

Diseases and insect pests that attack potatoes are too numerous to deal with here. Potato beetles, aphids and blight are just three of the scourges potatoes are susceptible to. However, modern research has developed various chemical and organic sprays and dusts to control most potato-growing problems. Consult your local Department of Agriculture for information on growing potatoes in your area.

Nutritional Value of the Potato

The potato is one of only a few foods capable of nourishing the great populations of the world. Contrary to popular belief, the potato is not fattening. A medium potato cooked with its skin contains only 90 calories (about the same as an apple or pear), yet supplies the following percentage of a recommended daily intake of nutrients:

Vitamin C =	30%
Iron =	8 to 10%
Thiamin (B$_1$) =	10%
Riboflavin (B$_2$) =	3%
Niacin =	11%
Protein =	3%
Calcium =	3%

Potato carbohydrate and iron is over 90 per cent usable. Complex carbohydrates such as those found in the potato are an essential part of a well-balanced diet. The ratio of protein to carbohydrate is higher in potatoes than in many cereals and the protein quality is higher than most other food crops.

A potato has about the same amount of Vitamin C as a glass of tomato juice; its iron content is equivalent to that found in an egg; and it is low in sodium and 99.9 per cent fat-free.

Many nutritionists agree that when starch is substituted for sugar, appetite is reduced; therefore potatoes, which also provide vitamins and minerals, are invaluable in reducing diets.

The following chart includes calorie counts of sample foods—note the low counts of most potato dishes. The measurement used is 3½ oz.

Food	Calories
Mashed potato	65
Boiled potato (peeled)	65
Whole milk	65
Potato (boiled in skin)	76
Potato (baked in skin)	93
Potato salad with dressing	99
Pork and Beans	122
Rice pudding with raisins	146
Ice Cream	207
Eggs, fried	216
Whiskey	249
Potatoes, French fried	274
Hamburger, regular	286
Boston Cream Pie	302
Chocolate Chiffon Cake	328
Yellow cake, chocolate icing	365
Choice club steak	380
Pecan Pie	418
Potato Chips	568
Bacon	611

Note: adding 1 tsp or a pat of butter to potatoes adds 35 calories.

Potato Varieties

Potatoes are available in a variety of colours, shapes and textures. The potato's appearance is related to its use. For example, long potatoes are best for baking, while round potatoes are best for boiling. This chart shows some of Canada's more widely used varieties.

Type	Variety
Russets	Russet Burbank (Netted Gem)
Round whites	Kennebec
	Sebago
	Superior
Reds	Chieftain
Yellow-fleshed	Bintje

Appearance and Texture

Uses

Oblong, slightly flattened lengthwise; lightly russeted, buff skin; white flesh; shallow eyes, fluffy texture produces light quality.

Best for mashed, baked, broiled and French fried potatoes; also in baked goods.

Round; smooth white skin; white flesh; slower to discolour than most other varieties so are most suitable when working with raw potatoes.

An all-purpose potato, best for boiled, baked and French-fried potatoes.

Round; smooth ivory-yellow skin; white flesh; a waxy potato that keeps its shape.

Best for boiling and in salads.

Round; smooth, white skin with a light flaky russet; white flesh.

Best for boiling.

Round; smooth bright-red skin; white flesh.

Best for boiling.

Long oval-shaped; large; smooth, pale yellow skin, shallow eyes; light yellow flesh.

Best for boiling, baking, French fries and potato chips.

Potato By-products

Potato starch is preferred by some cooks, rather than flour, as a thickener in sauces. When it is used, less simmering is required. However, it has no holding power, so foods thickened with potato starch must be served soon after thickening. One tablespoon of potato starch will thicken 1 cup of liquid to a moderate thickness.

Potato flour is a fine white flour made from cooked, dried potatoes. It is often used as a thickener in soups, sauces and stews. Potato flour has a taste of its own and should not be substituted for all-purpose flour. It can be used in breads, it can be mixed with another flour that has an adequate gluten content, or it can be used in some cakes and crackers for people on gluten-free diets.

Potato cheese is a German cheese made from cow's milk or occasionally sheep's or goat's milk. The milk is allowed to form a curd, then is added to boiled sieved potatoes along with salt and sometimes caraway seed. Cheeses are shaped, dried and covered with beer or cream before being set to ripen for two weeks.

The *potato chip* is one potato dish that is truly American. It is said to have been invented by a Native American, George Crum, of the Adirondack tribe. Crum was a chef at a popular spa, Moon's Lake House, at Saratoga Springs, New York in the mid-nineteenth century. Legend tells us he became upset when customers complained of the thickness of his fried potatoes. He cut the next batch paper thin with his razor. Whether this is true or not, the potato chip, originally called "Saratoga Chip," was born and today is North America's most popular snack food.

Potato chips are paper-thin slices of potato, soaked in cold water, then deep-fried in oil. They are then drained, seasoned and packaged. One store in New Hampshire devotes three entire aisles to various flavoured potato chips.

In the early 1960s, Premier Nikita Khrushchev of Russia was served potato chips on an American airplane. He then had a memo printed in *Pravda* in 1963, telling about the potato chip.

Potato Ice Cream is an all-natural sugar-free dairy product developed by Alan Reed of Idaho. In this new and innovative product, potato flakes are used as a stabilizing agent, and apple concentrate acts as the natural sweetener. Prince Edward Island businessmen Jack and Wes Sheridan are now attempting to produce Potato Ice Cream on the Island. Because the recipe has been written for mass quantities only, we are unable to include it here.

Buying and Storing Potatoes

Potatoes are graded and packaged under strict government regulations governing quality and size. Select potatoes that are firm, smooth, clean and uniform in shape, free from wrinkles, cuts, decay, blemishes or a green skin. Buy the size best suited to your needs.

Store potatoes in a cool, dry, well-ventilated place. The ideal temperature is 45 to 50°F. Be sure to store potatoes in a dark place as light causes greening and a bitter taste. This greening, caused by solanine, is mildly poisonous and if eaten may cause a headache or an upset stomach. There is no danger of poisoning from these potatoes, however, if the green areas are removed.

High temperatures may cause sprouting and shrivelling. Potatoes stored at room temperature should be used within a week.

Potatoes should never be stored in the refrigerator. Too cool temperatures will cause the starch in the potato to turn to sugar and give the potato an undesirable sweet taste. Potatoes that are too cold will also darken when cooked.

If possible, store potatoes in bins raised slightly from the floor to permit air to circulate. Potatoes are living and breathing. They must have air. Never store in a plastic bag or closed container.

If stored properly, potatoes will keep several months.

Potatoes on Prince Edward Island

Potato production in Canada is small in comparison with other countries, even though potatoes are grown in each of Canada's ten provinces. Prince Edward Island is Canada's smallest province (with a land mass of only 2,184 square miles), yet it ranks first in potato production, both in acres planted and in yield per acre.

In 1984, Prince Edward Island planted approximately 24 per cent of the potatoes planted in Canada and yielded just over 30 per cent of the total Canadian production.

Potatoes are the most important cash crop on Prince Edward Island, accounting for over one-third of the total farm cash receipts. This total amounts to more than the combined value of all other Island crops.

The first record of potato production in Prince Edward Island comes from a report sent to England by the colonial governor in 1771. By 1790, Island farmers were exporting small quantities of potatoes to Nova Scotia and New Brunswick. By 1830, exports were going to the West Indies. Because of transportation and road conditions at the time, it was actually easier and cheaper for some farmers in rural Prince Edward Island to ship their potatoes via a local port to the West Indies than to get them overland to market in Charlottetown.

Prince Edward Island was the first province in Canada to produce seed potatoes, shipping its first load in 1918.

Part of the reason for the potato's prosperity on Prince Edward Island is the red acidic, sandy, loam-type soil which contains large quantities of iron. As well, our growing season is one of warm days and cool nights with an average of 25mm of rain a week. These factors make ideal growing conditions for potatoes. Even our cold winter months and high snowfall help provide a natural control for many insects and diseases that could attack the potato. Being an island situated nine miles from the closest Canadian mainland insures that disease spores and insects cannot be introduced by air. Limited access points allow close monitoring of incoming vehicles associated with potato transportation.

There are nearly eight hundred potato growers on Prince Edward Island. All farmers growing over 0.1 hectares must notify the Potato

Marketing Board to ensure a disease control program is maintained.

The P.E.I. Potato Marketing Board was established in 1953. The board is made up of potato producers and dealers and is involved with promoting the production and marketing of high-quality potatoes, co-ordinating transportation, providing information on prices and market conditions, as well as administering the potato disease control program on behalf of the Elite Seed Farm.

The Elite Seed Farm, located on 350 acres of land at Fox Island (near Alberton, P.E.I.), has facilities equipped with automatically controlled temperature, humidity and ventilation for excellent potato storage. The farm operates a greenhouse and a well-equipped disease-testing laboratory. The aim of the farm is to produce high-quality, disease-resistant seed potatoes for its owners.

Most potatoes on Prince Edward Island are grown to seed standard, although not all of the crop that passes seed inspection is actually sold as seed. In 1985, 92 per cent of total acreage entered for seed inspection passed the inspection tests.

Prince Edward Island exports more than half of Canada's seed potatoes to over fifteen countries, including Argentina, Greece, Spain, Italy, Uruguay and Venezuela.

Most of the potato crop on Prince Edward Island is planted in May, although some farmers may plant in late April or on into early June, depending on soil and weather conditions. Potato farmers use a method of crop rotation, often on a three-year series with grain, rye grass or sometimes clover. Field soil is tested regularly to insure proper application level of fertilizers and lime. Many growers apply systemic insecticide and fertilizer at time of planting.

Potato farming is no easy business, and after the crop is in the ground growers must continually watch for insects and diseases, as well as follow a careful method of cultivation and spraying.

Potatoes are cultivated to control weeds and hilled to protect tubers from adverse weather conditions. Insecticides, herbicides and fungicides are used for control of insects, weeds or blight. The P.E.I. Department of Agriculture, the P.E.I. Potato Marketing Board and Agriculture Canada co-operate in a program of disease control. During the growing season, potato fields are closely monitored and inspected by government officials.

Potato plants must be dead before harvesting the tubers. Potatoes that are harvested when they are too green are very easily damaged and will not keep well. Most farmers apply a top killer to mature plants several days before harvest. This helps to control the size and prevent disease from spreading into the tubers.

Harvesting takes place in the cooler weather of early fall, usually beginning in September.

Some growers sell their potatoes directly from the field but most store their crop for later grading and marketing.

Potato storage must have ventilation, humidity and temperature under strict control. Potatoes are living and breathing, meaning that they can grow with air alone. Properly stored they will keep well up to ten months.

There are many difficulties in potato farming, with rising transportation costs, heavy costs of machinery, land shortages and marketing problems among them. In spite of these difficulties, Prince Edward Island has been named World Champion for both seed and tablestock potatoes at Canada's most prestigious agricultural exhibition—the Royal Winter Fair in Toronto, Ontario.

Easy or not, "As long as there's a 'Spud Island'—we'll be a growin' them" (P.E.I. Department of Agriculture).

The International Potato Centre

The International Potato Centre, herein called CIP from its Spanish name *Centro Internacional de La Papa,* is the hub of the world's potato research. The CIP, situated just outside Lima, Peru, is a non-profit scientific institution established in 1971 with the agreement of the government of Peru. It is funded by several foreign governments, regional organizations and private institutions, under the sponsorship of the World Bank. The goal of the CIP is "to develop improved agricultural technology, to increase food production and to improve the welfare of poor people in developing countries."

There are approximately four hundred people employed at the institute with several foreign anthropologists among the staff. The activities of the institute focus on research, training and dissemination of information on the potato. The centre has the world's most extensive collection of potato cultivars and exports seed tubers, seedlings, true potato seed and tissue culture to some eighty countries.

One of the programs from CIP, supported by the government of Ireland, provides a dry-food mix, made from three-tenths mashed potatoes combined with a mixture of available grains and legumes, that is given to school children as a dietary supplement. This mixture can be served in various ways, including a form of dessert.

The emblem of the CIP is a pre-Columbian deity holding a potato plant in each hand—one healthy and the other unhealthy. In 1981 a stamp was issued to commemorate the tenth anniversary of the centre.

Some of the recipes in this book have been adapted from a book compiled and published in 1978 by the CIP Women's Club. The book, written in both Spanish and English, is entitled *International Potato Cookery.*

The Potato Museum, Washington, D.C.

There are over twenty-five thousand museums around the world, yet, until 1975, none was dedicated solely to the potato.

Tom Hughes is founder and director of the world's first Potato Museum. He and his wife Meredith are curators of what *The New Yorker* called "one of the world's most exotic institutions."

Tom started the Potato Museum in Belgium in 1975 when he was employed as a fifth-grade teacher at the International School in Brussels. The museum grew steadily and in 1983 was moved to the United States. It is now situated in the Hughes' home on Capitol Hill, at 704 North Carolina Avenue, S.E., Washington, D.C.

The museum's collection now numbers over twenty-five hundred items, all of which cannot be displayed at once. However, the museum is open by appointment and visitors will find a fascinating variety of items on view. Included are songs, poems, books and major articles written about the potato, as well as ancient potato digging tools, mashers and peelers. There are bottles of potato liquors, toys, jewellery, postage stamps and even an 1828 "wanted" poster telling of a scoundrel from New Hampshire who stole a potato still. These and many more items form part of the world's most extensive collection of potato folklore.

A brochure from the museum states, "the museum aims to educate and entertain the public about this valuable plant while preserving items associated with its history and social influence."

Funding for the museum comes from $20 memberships which include a subscription to *Peelings,* the monthly newsletter. As well as editing the newsletter, Meredith Hughes spends much time in the museum kitchen trying recipes for "Potato Eaters' Night" which is a Wednesday night smorgasbord of potato dishes shared with friends. The museum is not funded with government assistance. The Hughes believe that one way of generating additional funding could be to open these dinners to the public.

Helpful Hints

A teaspoon of grated raw potato in a compress of surgical gauze is said to smooth eyelid wrinkles when placed over the closed eye for fifteen minutes.

To soften and remove blemishes from hands, make a paste from 1 medium cooked mashed potato, 1 tbsp safflower oil and a few drops of rose water. Apply to the hands, leave for 30 minutes and wash off. (This tip came to me from a penpal in Tasmania.)

Tired of oily skin? Blend ½ cup potatoes, peeled and grated, 1 egg white and 1 tbsp dry milk powder. Apply mixture to clean face. Leave 20 to 30 minutes. Wash off with warm water.

Raw potato is an old folk cure for cleansing the skin. "Rub a raw peeled potato on the skin directly or drink the juice regularly. This will cure eczema. Extract the juice with a liquidizer and mix with equal amounts of carrot juice to make it more palatable. Drink a glass a day."—Margaret Faulkner, Tasmania. (I have not tried the juice, but I have used raw potato to remove vegetable stains from my hands.)

A slice of raw potato will clean wood and silver.

A fun and simple activity for children is making potato prints. Cut a potato in half with a sharp knife. Carve out a picture or design, then dip in coloured ink and press on paper or fabric. Using paper grocery bags or inexpensive newsprint, children can make their own personalized gift wrap.

Don't throw away vitamins and minerals! Use leftover potato water in sauces, soups or baked goods.

¼ tsp cream of tartar added to the cooking water for the last 10 minutes will prevent potatoes from turning dark.

Too much salt in the soup? Add more potato. Simmer 30 minutes and discard the extra spuds.

Try adding mashed potatoes to your favourite recipes. Start by adding ½ cup to drop cookies, biscuits, fruit loaves or muffins. Potatoes help retain moisture in baked goods.

To thicken soups, add 3 tbsp grated raw potato for each cup of soup and simmer about 15 minutes.

The best method of cooking potatoes to preserve the maximum mineral content and taste is to bake them in hot coals or in the oven.

Don't waste potato peelings. The cortex of the potato, just below the skin, holds one-third of the potato's nutrients. If you must peel potatoes, peel them thinly.

Boiling potatoes in too much water or overcooking them will cause them to break up.

Baking potatoes without pricking the skin can cause an explosion in your oven.

Potatoes can be baked at 425°F for 40 to 50 minutes; at 375°F for 50 to 60 minutes or at 325°F for 75 minutes. Bake potatoes along with whatever else you may have in the oven.

Raw potatoes should never be stored in the refrigerator. Temperatures below 40°F will cause the starch in potatoes to convert to sugar. This produces an undesirable sweet flavour in cooked potatoes.

Try sprinkling some dry milk powder in a little potato water and add it to the potatoes as you mash them. Fast, economical and nutritious . . . and creamy mashed potatoes.

Potatoes begin to turn green when exposed to light—both sunlight and artificial light. To prevent this, store potatoes in a cool, dark place.

Remove all green areas found on potatoes before cooking. This green causes a bitter flavour in cooked potatoes and is mildly poisonous, often resulting in an upset stomach.

Potatoes can be baked in a covered coffee can or on an asbestos pad on top of a stove.

Too much fat on top of soup or gravy? Drop in a few large cold potato slices. The fat will cling to the cold potatoes which can then be discarded.

After deep frying, purify your fat by adding some thick slices of raw potato. Any taste of doughnuts, fish or onion, for example, will be absorbed by the potato, leaving the fat clear for the next time you use it.

If you burn your potatoes, scrape off the burnt part and put them in another pot. Add cold water and a speck of lemon juice and cook a few minutes longer. The burnt taste will be gone.

Is your sauce too thin? Add 1 tbsp potato starch and ½ cup cold water.

Add diced pimento to hot mashed potatoes for colour.

To keep mashed potatoes hot, cover and place the dish in a skillet of hot water.

Potatoes, unpeeled and boiled in salted water, do not absorb salt the way peeled potatoes do . . . important in some diets.

Potatoes that are boiled for about 5 minutes before baking will bake in half the usual time. Baking a potato with an aluminum skewer through it also cuts cooking time in half. (Don't try this method in a microwave though!)

Try oiling the skin of a potato before you bake it. The skins will be delicious.

To slice potatoes thinly, dip knife blade in boiling water.

To prevent potatoes from turning dark when peeled, put them in slightly salted water until ready to use. Or, add ascorbic acid to raw potatoes: dissolve 2-100 mg tablets of ascorbic acid in 2 tbsp water for each cup of potatoes.

For a new taste, cook potatoes in beef or chicken broth.

Prepare a "trim potato" scallop by replacing the whole milk with skim milk or broth.

For lower calories with baked potatoes, try a "Mock Sour Cream." Combine 1 cup cottage cheese, 1 tbsp lemon juice and ¼ cup water. Add salt to taste. Blend well.

Appetizers

For your next festive occasion, serve a variety of hot and cold appetizers: colourful dainties that are pleasing in texture and taste. As the beginning of a fancy luncheon or a pleasant ending to an evening out, appetizers are special "little somethings" that assure your friends you are glad they came. Served informally as help-yourself snacks, they can put your guests at ease.

Appetizers excite the appetite and set the stage for the meal to come. Try a "potato specialty" at your next party. The recipes included here are suitable for all occasions.

Crisp Potato Skins

Potato skins are fast becoming a popular snack food. They make an easy appetizer that are well worth trying. They're also great with soup.

6 medium baked potatoes or skins from leftover baked potatoes
½ cup melted butter or margarine
1 tsp garlic salt, celery salt or any desired seasoning salt
¼ cup grated parmesan or Swiss cheese

Preheat oven to 350°F. Cut baked potatoes into quarters. Scoop out pulp,* leaving only a thin layer of potato on each skin. Place skin side

down on a baking sheet and brush well with melted butter. Sprinkle with desired seasoning salt. Bake for 20 to 25 minutes until skins are brown and crisp. Sprinkle with cheese for the last 5 minutes of cooking period. Serve hot.
Serves 2 to 4.

Variations:

Before putting in the oven, any of the following toppings may be added:

1. 3 strips bacon, cooked crisp and crumbled mixed with ¼ cup grated cheddar cheese.
2. Equal amounts grated onion and green pepper, sautéed until tender in melted butter.
3. Fresh mushrooms, sliced and brushed with butter.

*Save the potato pulp for hash browns or mash and use in any one of the many baked products.

Party Potato Puffs

The potatoes for this recipe should be at room temperature. If they are not soft, add a little milk or water and beat.

1 cup mashed potato
½ cup sifted all-purpose flour
1 tsp double-acting baking powder
¼ tsp salt
1 slightly beaten egg
1 tsp parsley flakes
fat for pan frying (385°F)

Combine potato, flour, baking powder and salt. Add egg and parsley. Mix well. Drop by half-teaspoons into hot fat. Fry to a golden brown. Drain on absorbent paper. Serve hot.
Makes about 3 dozen appetizers.

The potato is the only vegetable to have a war named after it. That war was the Kartoffel Kreig (kartoffel = potato; kreig = war) of 1778–1779, also known as the War of the Bavarian Succession. Frederick the Great of Prussia was at odds with Austria. The armies ate one another's potatoes and, when cold weather set in, the fighting had to stop.

Potato Cheese Puffs

An attractive tempting potato dish.

2 beaten egg yolks
1⅓ cups mashed potato
3 tbsp hot milk
⅓ cup grated cheddar cheese
¼ tsp salt
¼ tsp paprika
¼ tsp celery salt
½ tsp finely minced onion
1 tsp chopped green pepper
2 stiffly beaten egg whites
1½ tbsp melted butter or margarine

Preheat oven to 350°F. Combine egg yolks, potato, milk, cheese, salt, paprika, celery salt, onion and green pepper. Mix well. Fold in beaten egg whites. Drop in mounds on a greased cookie sheet. Brush with melted butter. Bake for 20 minutes. Serve hot.
Makes 24 puffs; serves 6 to 8.

Potato Lemon Sticks

4 medium potatoes, unpeeled and cut in quarters
2 tsp lemon juice
2 tsp melted butter or margarine
2 tsp finely grated lemon peel
3 tbsp grated parmesan cheese
paprika

Preheat oven to 400°F. Mix together lemon juice and butter and brush on cut sides of the potato quarters. Combine lemon peel and cheese. Sprinkle over potatoes. Sprinkle with paprika. Place on a baking sheet. Bake for 30 to 35 minutes until potatoes are tender. Serve hot.
Serves 4 to 6.

Potatoes were planted in the Berlin Lustgarten in 1651 as an ornamental flower by Frederick the Great Elector. His grandson, Frederick William I, was convinced that potatoes had great nutritive value. He threatened to have the noses and ears cut off any of his subjects who refused to plant them.

Mexican Potato Puffs

These delicious appetizers may be made ahead and frozen for up to a month.

3 cups mashed potato
3 beaten eggs
1 tsp chili powder
⅛ tsp cayenne pepper
1 tsp salt
½ tsp dry mustard
1 tbsp grated onion
2 tsp milk
¾ cup grated cheddar cheese
¾ cup dry bread crumbs
fat for deep frying (400 to 450°F)

Combine all ingredients except cheese and bread crumbs. Chop cheese and crumbs in blender until fine. Add 1 cup to potato mixture. Shape in balls using one rounded tablespoon for each. Roll in remaining crumb mixture. Deep fry until golden brown. Serve hot.
Makes 48 puffs; serves 10 to 12.

Candied New Potatoes

A popular dish in China and Denmark.

18 to 20 medium new potatoes (not as large as mature potatoes)
½ cup brown sugar, packed
¼ cup water
2 tbsp butter or margarine
1 tsp salt
1 tbsp fresh dill

Boil and peel potatoes. Combine sugar, water, butter and salt. Cook over medium heat, stirring constantly until slightly thickened and bubbly. Reduce heat and stir in dill. Add potatoes and cook for 10 to 15 minutes. Stir potatoes in syrup to be sure they are evenly coated. They should glisten and be a rich brown colour. Serve hot.
Serves 6 to 8.

Frederick the Great of Prussia believed the best time for planting potatoes was in the dark of the moon.

Potato Peel Picks

4 medium potatoes
1 egg white
salt and pepper
dash of onion powder, garlic powder and oregano
2 tbsp parmesan cheese

Preheat oven to 475°F. Peel potatoes with fairly thick peels. Cut peels
in 2-inch slivers. Brush with egg white. Sprinkle with seasonings and
roll in cheese. Bake on a greased cookie sheet for 10 minutes. Toss to
make crisp on all sides. Serve hot.
Serves 4 to 6.

Pommes Dauphine

This is an original Jewish recipe despite the French name.

3 cups warm mashed potato
⅔ cup butter or margarine
¼ cup whipping cream
2 beaten egg yolks
1 cup water
1¼ tsp salt
1 cup all-purpose flour
4 eggs
fat for deep frying (370°F)

Combine potato with 4 tbsp butter, cream, egg yolks and 1 tsp salt. In
a saucepan heat water, remaining butter and ¼ tsp salt until butter
is melted and mixture is boiling rapidly. Add flour all at once. Remove
pan from the heat and stir in flour quickly. Hold pan above the heat
and stir mixture until the dough is thick and pulls away from the sides
of the pan to form a ball. Remove from heat. Add the eggs, one at a
time, beating well after each addition. Add potato and beat in well.
Drop by teaspoon into fat. Cook until they are lightly browned and
puffed. Drain on paper towels. Serve hot or cold.
Serves 8.

*The Indians of pre-Columbian Peru sometimes buried potato-shaped
stones in their potato beds to encourage regeneration.*

Potato Croquettes

A basic recipe with variations.

2 cups finely mashed potato
2 tbsp butter or margarine
½ tsp salt
⅛ tsp pepper
dash cayenne pepper
2 egg yolks
¼ tsp celery salt
1 tsp fresh chopped parsley

Combine all ingredients. Mix until soft and creamy. Chill 15 to 20 minutes to make easier to handle. Shape in balls by rolling one rounded tablespoon of mixture in handshape into a log shape.

Egg and Crumb Variation: Dip logs in a mixture of one beaten egg and 2 tbsp water. Coat with 1 cup sifted bread crumbs. Deep fry in fat at 390°F. Serve hot.
Serves 4.

Potato Apples Variation: Prepare croquettes, omitting pepper. Add 2 tbsp cream, ⅓ cup grated cheddar cheese and a dash of nutmeg. Shape like small apples. Roll in flour, then beaten egg, then sifted crumbs. Deep fry as above. Insert clove at stem end of each croquette. Serve hot.
Serves 6.

Heated Herbed Potato Chips

Preheat oven to 350°F. Spread potato chips on a cookie sheet. Top with shredded cheddar cheese. Sprinkle lightly with thyme, marjoram or basil. Heat for 5 minutes, until cheese melts. Serve hot.

People of Medieval Europe believed a potato in your pocket would prevent rheumatism. They thought that pregnant women who ate potatoes at night would give birth to children with large heads. They also believed that the placing of a potato skin at a young lady's door was an expression of contempt.

Potato Baskets

These dainty baskets are served with any desired filling. Creamed vegetables or fish are especially tasty.

3 cups hot mashed potato
1 tsp salt
3 tbsp butter or margarine
3 egg yolks, slightly beaten
2 tbsp milk or cream
1 egg white, slightly beaten

Preheat oven to 350°F. Combine potato, salt, butter, egg yolks and milk. Blend well. Shape into small baskets on greased cookie sheet, using a pastry bag and tube or a spoon. Brush with egg white and brown in oven. Fill while hot with desired filling.
Makes 12 baskets; serves 6.

Filling
2 tbsp butter or margarine
2 tbsp all-purpose flour
1 cup milk
salt to taste
chopped meat, flaked fish or cooked vegetables

Melt butter; stir in flour and salt. Gradually add milk. Cook over medium heat, stirring constantly until thickened. Add meat, fish or vegetables. Heat thoroughly.

Deep-Fried Potato Apples

tiny new potatoes (size of crab apples) or potato balls made with a melon scoop.
whole cloves
parsley
paprika
fat for deep frying (375°F)

Peel small potatoes. Soak in cold water for 15 minutes. Parboil 2 minutes and pat dry. Fry as for French fries. Insert a clove to represent the blossom end of an apple and put a sprig of parsley in the other end for a stem. Dust with paprika. Serve hot.

Salt Cod and Potato Nibblers

This recipe for these tasty bite-sized nibblers comes from the Prince Edward Island Department of Fisheries.

1 lb salt cod
2 tbsp melted butter or margarine
3 cups mashed potato
1 tbsp lemon juice
⅔ tsp onion salt
¼ tsp pepper
¼ tsp garlic salt
1 beaten egg
crushed cracker crumbs

Soak fish in cold water overnight. Boil in fresh water for 20 minutes. Drain and flake. Preheat oven to 450°F. Blend melted butter well with potato, fish, lemon juice, onion salt, pepper and garlic salt. Form into party balls and dampen with beaten egg. Roll in crushed cracker crumbs. Place on a well-greased baking sheet. Bake for 8 to 10 minutes or until browned and heated through. Serve hot.
Makes 36 nibblers.

Potato Fritters

2 cups hot mashed potato
2 tbsp white wine
2 tbsp cream
1 tsp salt
shake of nutmeg
3 well-beaten eggs
2 well-beaten egg yolks
½ cup all-purpose flour
dash cayenne pepper
fat for deep frying (375°F)

Combine potato, wine, cream, salt and nutmeg. Add eggs and egg yolks; place bowl in a larger bowl of iced water. Beat until cold. Add flour and cayenne pepper; mix well. Dip a metal spoon into hot fat, then spoon fritter batter into fat. Cook only 3 to 4 fritters at a time. Cook 3 to 5 minutes, until a delicate brown colour. Drain on absorbent paper. Serve hot.
Serves 8.

Potato-Roma Snacks

5 to 6 medium potatoes, boiled and mashed
2 egg yolks
½ cup grated parmesan cheese
2 tbsp vegetable oil
2 tbsp chopped onion
¼ cup chopped fresh parsley
1 tsp salt
1 tsp garlic salt
½ tsp pepper
¾ cup all-purpose flour
2 beaten eggs
1 cup fine dry bread crumbs
fat for deep frying (375°F)

Add egg yolks and cheese to mashed potato. Mix well. Sauté onion in
oil until tender. Add to potato mixture; stir in parsley, salt, garlic salt
and pepper. Stir until smooth. Shape into small balls (1 rounded tsp
for each ball). Roll in flour, dip in egg, then roll in bread crumbs.
Deep fry until brown in hot oil. Snacks may be refrigerated, or frozen
and thawed at room temperature then reheated in a slow oven. Serve hot.
Serves 6 to 8.

Cindy's Party Snacks

Cindy Chase of Halifax shared this recipe with me.

2 cups hot mashed potato
2 tbsp chopped mint leaves
¼ tsp paprika
½ tsp salt
2 tbsp butter or margarine
1 egg yolk
1 egg white, slightly beaten
2 tbsp water
1 cup sifted bread crumbs
fat for deep frying (350°F)

Combine potato, mint, paprika, salt, butter and egg yolk. Shape in
small balls. Dilute slightly beaten egg white with 2 tbsp water. Dip
balls in liquid. Roll in crumbs and deep fry until brown. Serve hot.
Makes approximately 24 party snacks.

Potato and Fish Tidbits

Use whatever fish you have on hand. Potatoes blend equally well with cod, bluefish and salmon, to name a few.

1 lb cooked fish, drained and flaked
3 cups mashed potato
2 tbsp melted butter or margarine
1 small onion, very finely chopped
1 tsp salt
¼ tsp pepper
1 tbsp lemon juice
1 beaten egg
1 cup dry bread crumbs (approx.)
fat for deep frying (350°F)

Combine fish, potato, butter, onion, salt, pepper and lemon juice. Mix well. Form into bite-sized balls. Dip in beaten egg and roll in bread crumbs. Deep fry in fat for 2 to 3 minutes. Drain on absorbent paper. Serve hot.
Serves 10 to 12.

Mini Seafood Quiches

1 recipe potato pastry
1 cup canned mackerel
¼ cup finely chopped onion
1 cup grated Swiss cheese
2 beaten eggs
1 cup light cream
2 tbsp parsley flakes
½ tsp salt
pinch of pepper
paprika

Preheat oven to 350°F. Prepare pastry. Roll out and cut into circles for lining muffin tins. Drain fish and flake into a bowl. Combine onion and cheese. Fill tart shells ⅔ full with mackerel mixture. Beat eggs, cream, parsley, salt and pepper until well-blended. Spoon egg mixture into each tart shell being careful not to fill too full. Sprinkle with paprika. Bake for 40 minutes until a knife inserted in the centre comes out clean. Serve hot.
Makes 12 mini quiches.

Salmon-Potato Mini Puffs

2 egg whites
2 egg yolks
1 small can salmon (8 oz)
1½ cups mashed potato
2 tbsp mayonnaise
1 tbsp chopped fresh parsley
¼ tsp lemon rind
salt and pepper to taste
dash of onion salt

Preheat oven to 375°F. Beat egg whites to stiff peaks and set aside.
Combine all other ingredients. Fold in egg whites. Spoon tablespoons
of batter into small balls. Set in a shallow pan of water and oven poach
for 20 minutes. Serve hot.
Serves 6 to 8.

*How did potatoes, one of the world's great health-giving foods, get the
name "spud"? One story goes that when potatoes were first introduced
in Europe, the mainstay of life was grain. The large milling industry,
fearful of competition from potatoes, did everything possible to discourage
the consumption of potatoes. They organized societies to dissuade people
from eating the new tubers. The groups were called "The Society to
Prevent Unhealthy Diets": hence, "spud."*

Breakfasts

Want something different for breakfast? Why not serve potatoes? Potatoes combine well with a variety of ingredients to make delicious and nutritious breakfasts. Pancakes, soufflés, omelettes and quiche are just a few of the tempting potato breakfasts you'll find in this chapter.

Potato Farmer's Breakfast

¼ lb bacon
3 cups cubed cooked potato
1 cup chopped onion
2 tbsp chopped chives
6 eggs, beaten
½ tsp salt
¼ tsp pepper
½ cup grated cheddar cheese

Fry bacon in a large frying pan. Drain fat. Add cubed potato, onion and chives. Cook 5 minutes. Stir in beaten eggs, salt and pepper. Sprinkle grated cheese over mixture. Cover and cook over moderate heat for an additional 5 minutes. Cut in wedges to serve.
Serves 6.

Savory Country-Style Scramble

Potatoes team up with bacon and eggs for a special brunch. Serve with tomato slices and green beans.

3 slices bacon
1 tbsp oil
2 cups diced raw potato
¼ cup chopped onion
⅛ tsp savory
4 eggs
1 tbsp water
¼ tsp salt
dash pepper
¼ cup diced cheese

Fry bacon in large frying pan, retaining drippings. Crumble and set aside. Add oil, potato, onion and savory to bacon drippings. Cover and cook over low heat, stirring frequently, until potato is tender (approximately 30 minutes). Stir in crumbled bacon. Blend eggs, water, salt and pepper. Pour over the potato mixture and cover. When partly set, lift and turn in sections. Sprinkle cheese on top; cover and cook for 3 minutes or until cheese is melted. Serve at once.
Serves 4.

German Winterland Delight

A quick, satisfying breakfast or supper dish.

6 slices bacon
2 tbsp chopped onion
3 large boiled potatoes, cubed
salt and pepper to taste
6 eggs
grated cheese (optional)

Fry bacon over low heat until brown and crisp; cut into small pieces. Fry onion, potatoes, bacon, salt and pepper in bacon fat and cook until potatoes are browned. Stir often. Break eggs into pan over top of potatoes. Cover and cook over low heat until eggs are set. Sprinkle with grated cheese if desired, either before or after eggs are added. Serve hot.
Serves 6.

Baked Eggs in Potato Boats

A great breakfast as well as an easy lunch on a lazy day.

3 large baked potatoes
3 tbsp butter
½ tsp salt
⅛ tsp pepper
¼ cup hot milk
6 eggs

Preheat oven to 350°F. Cut potatoes in half lengthwise and scoop out pulp. Be careful not to break the potato skins. Mash potatoes; add butter, salt, pepper and milk. Beat until light and fluffy. Spoon into potato shells, leaving a hollow in each. Break an egg in each hollow. Season with additional salt and pepper if desired, and bake until eggs are firm.
Serves 6.

Saucy Egg and Potato Patties

2 cups mashed potato
salt and pepper to taste
¼ cup grated cheddar cheese
butter or margarine for frying
1½ cups cooked tomato
¼ cup chopped onion
6 eggs

Combine potato, salt, pepper and cheese. Shape mixture into six patties and brown in skillet in butter. Cook tomato and onion until thick. Fry eggs and place one egg on each potato pattie. Cover with tomato sauce. Serve at once.
Makes 6 servings.

Many people rejected potatoes because they "wanted no truck with anything that grew underground."

In 1619, the potato was banned in Burgundy, France. It was believed to cause leprosy, a misconception that lasted well into the eighteenth century.

Fisherman's Delight

A great breakfast at home or on your next camping trip. Tastes especially good if you are lucky enough to have fresh trout.

4 well-beaten eggs
1 cup milk
1 cup mashed potato
1 cup all-purpose flour
1 small onion, finely chopped
fat for frying

Mix all ingredients. Pour in just enough batter to barely cover bottom of frying pan. Cook a few minutes and turn over as you would pancakes. Serve with maple syrup and bacon, sausage or trout.
Serves 4.

Meat-and-Potato Quiche

An attractive dish with its browned crispy potato edging.

3 tbsp vegetable oil
3 cups coarsely grated raw potato
1 cup grated cheddar or Swiss cheese
¾ cup cooked diced meat (ham, chicken or sausage)
¼ cup chopped onion
1 cup evaporated milk
2 eggs
½ tsp salt
⅛ tsp pepper
1 tbsp parsley flakes

Preheat oven to 425°F. Combine vegetable oil and grated potato. Press evenly into a 9-inch pie plate to form a pie crust. Bake for 15 minutes until it begins to brown. Remove from oven. Cover potato crust with cheese, meat, and onion in layers. Mix together milk, eggs, salt and pepper. Pour over other ingredients. Sprinkle with parsley. Bake 30 minutes until knife inserted in centre comes out clean. Cool 5 minutes before cutting.
Serves 6.

The Inca Indians measured time by how long it took potatoes to cook.

Cheesy Potato Soufflé

2 cups mashed potato, slightly cooled
4 slices cooked ham, cut in small cubes
½ cup grated cheddar cheese
6 egg yolks
½ tsp salt
pinch pepper
6 egg whites

Preheat oven to 325°F. Combine mashed potato, ham and cheese; mix well. Beat egg yolks, add to potato mixture. Stir in salt and pepper; beat until light and fluffy. In a large bowl, beat egg whites until they form stiff peaks. Gently fold egg whites into potato mixture. Place in a 1½-quart ungreased casserole and bake for 25 minutes, until puffed and golden brown. Serve at once.
Makes 6 servings.

Potato Omelette

A delightful way to start the day!

3 egg yolks
3 tbsp cream
1 cup mashed potato
1 tsp salt
¼ tsp pepper
1 tbsp finely grated onion
chopped fresh parsley
3 egg whites
butter

Preheat oven to 350°F. Combine egg yolks, cream and potato; beat until smooth. Season to taste with salt, pepper, grated onion and parsley. Beat egg whites until stiff. Fold into potato mixture. Place in a buttered casserole dish or skillet. Bake until brown (approximately 10 to 15 minutes). Fold and turn onto a hot serving platter. Serve at once.
Serves 4 to 6.

The word "boycott" came from the time when Captain Boycott's tenants refused to dig potatoes and other crops for him. Their rebellion was on September 22, 1873.

Potato Pepperoni Omelette

This omelette takes a bit longer to make than most. Try it for a Sunday brunch and enjoy a taste of Spain. Prepare omelette in a large electric frying pan or any covered frying pan.

2 tbsp butter or margarine
2 tbsp olive oil
1¼ cups finely diced raw potato
½ cup chopped Spanish onion
½ cup sliced mushrooms
1 clove garlic, minced
8 eggs
salt to taste
dash crushed red pepper
½ cup chopped pepperoni

Heat butter and oil over medium heat. Add potato and cook until tender, about 15 minutes. Stir often to distribute heat evenly. Add onion, mushrooms and garlic. Cook another few minutes until tender. Beat eggs, salt and pepper; combine with pepperoni. Add to the vegetable mixture. Cover and cook 4 to 5 minutes until slightly set. Flip omelette and cook other side for another 4 minutes. Serve hot.
Serves 8.

Grated-Potato Pancakes

3 cups raw potato, grated
2 eggs, beaten
1 cup milk
½ cup finely minced onion
¼ cup all-purpose flour
2 tsp baking powder
1 tsp salt
fat for frying

Drain liquid from grated potato. Combine eggs, milk and onion. Sift dry ingredients and add to mixture. Fold in potato. Melt a little fat in a skillet and cook pancakes in 1/3 cup amounts. Brown on both sides, turning once. Serve hot with applesauce.
Makes 10 pancakes.

Potato Pancakes I

Made with leftover mashed potato, these quickly prepared pancakes are a family favourite at our house.

1 cup mashed potato
2 cups sifted all-purpose flour
1 tsp salt
3 tsp baking powder
1 tsp nutmeg
2 eggs, beaten
1 cup milk (approx.)
¼ cup light corn syrup

Combine potato, sifted flour, salt, baking powder and nutmeg. Mix together eggs and milk; stir lightly into potato-flour mixture. Add corn syrup and beat well. If batter is too thick you may need to add a bit more milk. Brown on both sides on a greased griddle, turning once. Serve with Potato Maple Syrup (see Miscellaneous).
Serves 6.

Potato Pancakes II

These pancakes are served with ham, sausage, bacon or eggs for breakfast or brunch. They can be accompanied by sour cream, maple syrup, apple sauce or any desired pancake topping.

3 cups grated raw potato
6 tbsp milk
3 tbsp all-purpose flour
¼ tsp baking powder
1 egg
1 small onion, grated finely
1 tsp salt
fat for greasing skillet

Combine all ingredients except fat. Pour in small amounts on a hot greased skillet. Brown on both sides, turning once.
Serves 6.

"Tu me dices papas."—*A Spanish expression meaning "you're fibbing" or, literally translated, "you are telling me potatoes."*

Peruvian Potato Pancakes

A recipe for a big family breakfast. Makes light and fluffy pancakes.
Serve with Potato Maple Syrup (see Miscellaneous).

1½ cups all-purpose flour
1 cup mashed potato
5 tsp baking powder
1 tsp salt
3 tbsp granulated sugar
2 eggs
2 cups milk
⅓ cup oil
fat for frying

Preheat a large frying pan (if using an electric one, heat to 375°F). Put
all ingredients in a blender. Mix only until smooth and free of lumps.
Do not overmix. (I find putting the liquid ingredients in first makes a
better batter.) Grease frying pan lightly and cook pancakes in ¼ cup
amounts. When top side of pancake bubbles, turn over and brown other
side. Serve hot.
Makes 30 pancakes.

Potato-Carrot Pancakes

4 eggs
2 cups raw potato, finely grated
2 cups raw carrot, finely grated
1 tbsp onion, chopped
2 tbsp all-purpose flour
1¼ tsp salt
¼ tsp baking powder
¼ tsp dill seed (optional)
oil for frying

Beat eggs. Add potato, carrot, onion and dry ingredients. Mix
thoroughly. Pour in ¼ cup portions on moderately hot frying pan. Flatten with spatula. Fry until crisp and browned; turn and cook until
other side is browned. If necessary, drain pancakes on paper towel. Add
oil to pan before making each set of pancakes. Serve hot with sour cream.
Serves 6.

Holiday Potato Pancakes

A potato pancake with a difference: finely chopped cooked turkey is added to the batter. Pancakes can be served with cranberry sauce. Special for a Boxing Day brunch.

3 medium grated raw potatoes (about 2½ cups)
1 tsp salt
dash pepper
2 eggs, beaten
2 tbsp all-purpose flour
1 tbsp finely chopped onion
1 cup finely chopped cooked turkey
fat for frying

Combine all ingredients. Drop by spoonfuls on lightly oiled hot skillet. Fry until brown on one side, then turn and brown other side. Serve hot with cranberry sauce or maple syrup.
Serves 4 to 6.

Old South Potato Corn Pudding

Canned corn gives a new twist to leftover potatoes. A popular quiche-like Sunday brunch dish that is ready in just 30 minutes.

1 tbsp butter or margarine
2 cups cooked potato, cut in small cubes
2 green onions, sliced (use entire onion)
1 cup whole kernel corn, drained
¾ tsp salt
½ tsp thyme
¼ tsp pepper
1¼ cups milk
2 eggs, beaten
paprika

Preheat oven to 375°F. Melt butter to sizzling in large pan. Add potato and onion. Cook and stir for 5 minutes. Mix in corn, salt, thyme, pepper and milk. Remove from heat. Stir in eggs until thoroughly blended. Pour into a greased 9-inch pie plate or quiche dish. Dust with paprika. Bake 15 to 18 minutes, until set. Cut in wedges to serve. Leftovers may be refrigerated and served chilled or reheated in a microwave oven.
Serves 4 to 6.

Quick Breads

The nicest thing about quick breads is just that—they are quick. For a special breakfast, when unexpected guests drop in or to share when a friend has a problem, quick breads say without words, "I made something special just for you."

Quick breads are leavened with baking powder, baking soda and eggs rather than yeast (leaving a distinctive crack down the centre). They include a delicate array of biscuits, scones, muffins, dumplings, doughnuts, pancakes and fruit loaves. Except for the fruit loaves that require aging, quick breads are best served hot. Most quick breads freeze well and can be wrapped in foil and easily reheated to serve.

There is something special about hot biscuits or scones served with butter and jam. Tea breads spread with butter or creamed cheese make welcome additions to lunch boxes. What better way to start the day than with spicy muffins, fresh from the oven.

Here you will find a varied selection of all these and more.

A statue of Sir Francis Drake holding a potato plant once stood in Offenburg, West Germany. It was erected in 1853 to honour the man credited with bringing the potato to Europe. Around the statue's base were garlands of potato leaves and inscriptions of thanks. The statue was destroyed in 1939.

Potato Bannock

Bannock is the Gaelic word for cake. It is also called "Cake Bread." There are over one hundred kinds of bannock. An old superstition says, "If you eat bannock on Halloween your dreams will foretell your future."

2⅓ cups all-purpose flour
1 tsp salt
2 tbsp baking powder
4 tbsp sugar
2 tbsp shortening or lard
¾ cup mashed potato
1 cup cold potato water or water

Preheat oven to 450°F. Sift flour, salt, baking powder and sugar. Cut in shortening until mixture resembles coarse meal. Stir in potato. Add cold water and mix with a fork. Knead gently 8 or 10 times on a lightly floured board. Use extra flour if necessary. Pat into an oval shape about ¾ inch thick. Score with a sharp knife. Bake for 20 minutes or until bannock sounds hollow when tapped. Serve with butter, and jam or molasses.
Serves 8.

Sweet Biscuits

These biscuits that use equal amounts of mashed potato and all-purpose flour are my husband's favourite. They can be served plain or made with a large cookie cutter and used for strawberry shortcake.

2 cups all-purpose flour
4 tsp baking powder
¾ tsp salt
¼ cup granulated sugar
½ cup shortening or margarine
2 cups mashed potato
⅔ cup milk, approximately (depending on the wetness of the potatoes)

Preheat oven to 400°F. Combine flour, baking powder, salt and sugar. Cut in shortening. Stir in potato and mix thoroughly. Add enough milk to make a soft dough. Knead lightly on a floured board. Cut with a biscuit cutter. Bake on a greased cookie sheet for 15 minutes. Serve hot.
Makes 24 biscuits.

Potato Biscuits

These biscuits are quick to make and bake in only 15 minutes.

1½ cups all-purpose flour
1 tbsp baking powder
1 tsp salt
2 tbsp shortening
½ cup cold mashed potato
½ cup cold milk

Preheat oven to 400°F. Combine flour, baking powder and salt. Cut in shortening. Add potato and mix thoroughly. Add enough milk to make a soft dough. Roll lightly to ½-inch thickness. Cut with biscuit cutter. Bake 12 to 15 minutes. Serve hot.
Makes 12 biscuits.

Dutch Biscuits

Of the many recipes for Potato biscuits I tested while researching this book, Dutch Biscuits were unanimously voted Number One.

3 cups all-purpose flour
1 cup brown sugar
1 tsp salt
2 tsp cinnamon
1 tsp baking soda
3 tsp baking powder
¾ cup shortening
2 cups mashed potato
1 cup raisins
1 egg, slightly beaten
1 cup sour milk

Preheat oven to 425°F. Combine flour, brown sugar, salt, cinnamon, baking soda and baking powder. Cut in shortening with a pastry blender until mixture resembles coarse meal. Add mashed potato and raisins. Toss lightly until potato is well-mixed into dry ingredients. Combine slightly beaten egg and sour milk. Add to other ingredients, mixing lightly with a fork. Pat to 1-inch thickness. Cut with a biscuit cutter. Place on greased cookie sheet. Lightly brush tops with milk if a shiny top is desired. Bake 15 to 18 minutes.
Makes 24 biscuits.

Chocolate Potato Doughnuts

This recipe comes from Carol Ann Newson of Summerside, P.E.I.

2 eggs
1 cup granulated sugar
3 squares unsweetened chocolate
2 tbsp shortening
1 cup mashed potato
3½.cups sifted all-purpose flour
6 tsp baking powder
1 tsp salt
¼ tsp cinnamon
⅔ cup milk
fat for deep frying (375°F)

Beat eggs until light, gradually adding sugar. Melt together unsweetened chocolate and shortening. Add potato and chocolate to first
mixture. Sift dry ingredients. Fold in dry ingredients alternately with
milk. Use just enough flour to make a dough that can be easily handled.
Chill in refrigerator at least one hour. Roll to ½-inch thickness on a
lightly floured board. Cut with a doughnut cutter. Deep fry in hot fat
until brown on both sides, turning once after about 45 seconds. Drain
on absorbent paper.
Makes 3 dozen doughnuts.

Double-Chocolate Variation: For double-chocolate doughnuts spread
slightly cooled doughnuts with a chocolate glaze.

Chocolate Glaze
1 oz semi-sweet chocolate
2 tbsp butter or margarine
2 tbsp milk
1 cup icing sugar
¼ tsp vanilla
⅛ tsp salt

Melt chocolate. Add remaining ingredients. Blend well.

"If a man really likes potatoes, he must be a decent sort of fellow . . ."
—*A.A. Milne*

Fluffy Potato Doughnuts

Definitely the lightest doughnut you will ever taste.

3 eggs
1⅓ cups granulated sugar
½ tsp vanilla
1 cup cooled mashed potato
2 tbsp melted shortening
4 cups all-purpose flour
6 tsp baking powder
2 tsp nutmeg
1 tsp salt
½ cup milk
fat for deep frying (375°F)

Beat eggs with sugar and vanilla until light. Add potato and shortening and blend well. Sift together dry ingredients; add alternately with milk to potato mixture, beginning and ending with flour. Beat well. Chill 1½ hours. Heat fat for frying. While fat is heating, roll out half the dough at a time, keeping the remainder chilled. Roll to approximately ½-inch thickness. Cut with floured doughnut cutter. Deep fry in fat for about 3 minutes, turning once. Drain. Dip in sugar or a mixture of sugar and cinnamon. Best if served warm.
Makes 3 dozen doughnuts.

Lemon Loaf

Light and delicious, this recipe makes a large loaf.

⅓ cup shortening
⅓ cup mashed potato
1 cup granulated sugar
2 eggs, beaten
rind of one lemon, grated finely
1 tsp baking powder
½ tsp baking soda
½ tsp salt
½ cup milk
1½ cups all-purpose flour
juice of a half-lemon mixed with ⅓ cup granulated sugar (for glaze)

Preheat oven to 350°F. Grease a 13x4-inch loaf pan and line with waxed paper. Cream shortening and mashed potato. Gradually add sugar, blending well. Add eggs and lemon rind. Mix well. Sift dry ingredients and add alternately with milk, beginning and ending with dry ingredients. Mix well after each addition. Bake in prepared pan for 1 hour. Remove from oven. Spread glaze over loaf. Let stand 10 minutes. Invert on rack; remove waxed paper. Set on another cake rack in upright position to cool completely before cutting.

Nut Loaf

Good old-fashioned flavour — rich and tender. From the P.E.I. Potato Marketing Board.

2 cups all-purpose flour
1 tsp cocoa
2 tsp baking powder
1 tsp baking soda
¼ tsp salt
1 cup mashed potato
½ cup milk
½ cup butter or margarine
2 cups granulated sugar
1 tsp vanilla
1 cup finely chopped walnuts
3 egg whites

Grease and flour two 9x5-inch loaf pans. Preheat oven to 350°F. Combine flour, cocoa, baking powder, baking soda and salt; set aside. Beat potato and milk until no lumps remain. Cream butter and sugar until light. Add vanilla. Blend in dry ingredients gradually, alternating with potato/milk mixture, beginning and ending with dry ingredients. Fold in nuts. Beat egg whites until light and fold in. Pour batter in prepared pans. Bake 30 minutes until toothpick inserted in centre comes out dry.

There are as many as three hundred seeds in one potato berry. Seven hundred thousand potato seeds weigh approximately one pound. A small glass jar of True Potato Seed is equivalent in crop potential to two tons of seed potatoes.

Potato Cherry-Nut Loaf

The batter is a bit wetter than other loaves.

3 tbsp butter or margarine
1 cup granulated sugar
½ cup mashed potato
2 eggs
¼ tsp almond flavouring
2¼ cups all-purpose flour
3 tbsp baking powder
½ tsp salt
¼ cup maraschino cherry juice
¾ cup milk
1 cup maraschino cherries, halved
½ cup chopped walnuts

Preheat oven to 350°F. Grease a 13x4-inch loaf pan and line with waxed paper. Cream butter, sugar and potato. Add eggs and flavouring and beat well. Combine dry ingredients. Stir cherry juice into milk. Add dry ingredients and liquids to first mixture alternately, beginning and ending with dry ingredients. Blend well. Stir in cherries and nuts. Spoon into prepared pan. Bake 1 hour or until toothpick inserted in centre comes out clean.

Sugar-Glazed Orange-Potato Loaf

The addition of mashed potato gives this loaf a lovely, moist texture.

⅓ cup shortening
1 cup granulated sugar
2 beaten eggs
1 tbsp finely grated orange rind
juice of one orange
1 tsp baking powder
½ tsp baking soda
½ tsp salt
1¾ cups all-purpose flour
½ cup mashed potato
½ cup milk
¼ cup granulated sugar

Preheat oven to 350°F. Grease a 9x5-inch loaf pan and line with waxed paper. Combine shortening, sugar, eggs, orange rind and half the orange juice. Beat with an electric mixer until well-blended. In another bowl mix baking powder, baking soda, salt, flour and potato. Toss lightly to evenly distribute potato through the dry ingredients. Make a well in centre of dry ingredients and add shortening mixture and milk. Mix until blended. Bake 1 hour. Remove from oven. Combine remaining orange juice and ¼ cup granulated sugar. Spread over loaf. Let stand a few minutes. Remove loaf from pan, remove waxed paper and set loaf in an upright position to cool.

Potato Fruit-and-Nut Bread

¼ cup melted butter or margarine
1 cup granulated sugar
2 well-beaten eggs
1 tbsp finely grated orange rind
1 cup slightly warmed mashed potato
2 cups all-purpose flour
3 tsp baking powder
1 tsp baking soda
½ tsp salt
1 cup raisins
¾ cup chopped walnuts
½ cup milk

Preheat oven to 350°F. Grease a 9x5-inch loaf pan and line with waxed paper. Combine butter and sugar and blend well. Add beaten eggs, orange rind and potato. Blend thoroughly. Sift dry ingredients and mix with raisins and nuts. Add to butter-and-egg mixture alternately with milk. Blend well. Bake 1 hour or until toothpick inserted in centre comes out clean.

One of the newer "potato items" to be found is the potato clock. Invented by Bill Borst of Elon College in North Carolina, it is made to run on two potatoes. Copper and zinc probes are inserted in the potato and are said to cause enough flow of electrons to power the clock. The one in my office will run for ten to twelve weeks without changing potatoes. Incidentally, it keeps perfect time.

Potato-Bran Bread

High in iron and fibre. Serve with vegetable dishes or in lunch boxes. This recipe makes a large loaf.

1 cup bran
½ cup whole wheat flour
¾ cup all-purpose flour
1 tbsp baking powder
½ tsp baking soda
1 tsp salt
⅓ cup granulated sugar
½ cup raisins
1 egg, well-beaten
¼ cup molasses
1 cup milk
¾ cup potato, cooked and mashed well

Preheat oven to 375°F. Grease a 9x5-inch loaf pan. Mix dry ingredients and raisins. Combine liquids and potato and beat with electric mixer until lumps are gone. Add dry ingredients to liquid and mix together. Fill loaf pan two-thirds full. Bake 1 hour. Allow to cool before cutting.

Cornmeal Muffins

1 cup cornmeal
1 cup sour milk
½ cup all-purpose flour
¼ cup granulated sugar
½ tsp baking soda
2 tsp baking powder
½ cup mashed potato
1 egg, beaten
3 tbsp vegetable oil

Mix together cornmeal and sour milk. Set aside for 10 minutes. Preheat oven to 400°F. Combine flour, sugar, baking soda and baking powder. Add mashed potato to cornmeal mixture. Mix in egg and oil and beat with an electric mixer until smooth. Make a well in centre of dry ingredients and add cornmeal mixture all at once. Stir quickly until ingredients are just mixed and batter is lumpy in appearance. Fill greased muffin tins two-thirds full and bake 15 to 20 minutes.
Makes 12 muffins.

Applesauce-Date Muffins

A light tasty muffin for breakfast or snacks.

½ cup butter or margarine
1 cup firmly packed brown sugar
1 egg
1½ cups all-purpose flour
1 tsp baking powder
1 tsp baking soda
½ tsp salt
½ tsp cinnamon
½ cup finely chopped dates
½ cup riced potato
¾ cup unsweetened applesauce

Preheat oven to 375°F. Grease or line muffin tins. Cream together butter and brown sugar; beat in egg. Sift dry ingredients. Combine dates and potato with flour mixture. Stir into batter alternately with applesauce. Mix just until blended. Fill muffin tins two-thirds full. Bake 20 minutes.
Makes 12 large muffins.

Date-Nut Muffins

This recipe uses the water drained from cooking potatoes to make a fine-textured light muffin.

1 cup chopped dates
1 cup boiling potato water
3 tbsp butter or margarine
1 cup brown sugar
1 egg, well-beaten
1 tsp vanilla
½ cup chopped walnuts
1¾ cups all-purpose flour
1 tsp baking soda
¼ tsp salt

Preheat oven to 350°F. Grease or line muffin tins. Combine dates, potato water and butter and let cool. Blend in sugar, egg, vanilla and nuts. Sift flour, baking soda and salt and stir into batter. Fill greased muffin tins two-thirds full. Bake 20 to 25 minutes.
Makes 18 muffins.

Best-Ever Blueberry Muffins

These muffins are so moist and flavourful, buttering them isn't necessary.

1 cup buttermilk
¼ cup vegetable
¾ cup granulated sugar
2 eggs, beaten
2 cups all-purpose flour
1½ tsp baking powder
1½ tsp baking soda
⅛ tsp nutmeg
½ tsp salt
1 cup mashed potato
1 cup fresh blueberries

Preheat oven to 400°F. Grease or line muffin tins. Combine buttermilk, oil, sugar and eggs. Mix well. Sift flour, baking powder, baking soda, nutmeg and salt. Toss blueberries and mashed potatoes in flour mixture. Stir lightly into other ingredients. Mix only until blended. Pour into greased muffin tins, filling three-quarters full. Bake 15 to 20 minutes. *Makes 18 muffins.*

Old-Fashioned English-Potato Muffins

Quick to make on a griddle.

1 cup all-purpose flour
4 tsp baking powder
½ tsp salt
1 tbsp granulated sugar
⅛ tsp nutmeg
2 tbsp shortening
½ cup cold mashed potato
⅓ cup milk (approximate)

Sift together in a mixing bowl flour, baking powder, salt, sugar and nutmeg. Cut in shortening until the mixture resembles a coarse meal. Mash cold potato until smooth. Stir into flour mixture. Make a well in centre and add milk. Mix lightly with a fork, adding a bit more milk if necessary to make a soft dough. Turn onto a lightly floured board and knead until smooth. Pat or roll to ½-inch thickness or less. Cut

with a 3-inch cookie cutter. Dust a griddle with flour and heat until flour browns slightly. Bake muffins on moderately hot griddle until cooked through and golden brown, turning once (12 to 15 minutes). Serve hot with butter, honey or jam.
Makes about 12 muffins.

Oatmeal-Potato Muffins

1 cup quick-cooking rolled oats
1 cup buttermilk
¾ cup cold mashed potato
½ cup brown sugar
1 egg
½ cup vegetable oil
1 tsp vanilla
1 cup all-purpose flour
1 tsp baking powder
½ tsp baking soda
½ tsp cinnamon
½ tsp nutmeg
½ tsp salt
1 cup raisins

Grease or line muffin tins. Combine rolled oats and buttermilk and let stand 1 hour. Preheat oven to 400°F. Add potato, sugar, egg, vegetable oil and vanilla. Blend well. Sift flour, baking powder, baking soda, cinnamon, nutmeg and salt; add raisins. Gradually add to other mixture stirring only until blended. Pour into muffin tins. Bake 15 to 20 minutes.
Makes 18 muffins.

As part of a diet study done by New Jersey's Dr. Oscar Kruesi some years ago, twenty-three men were given ten potatoes per day, which they could have prepared in any form except French fries or potato chips. "After three months of eating ten potatoes a day, the average man had lost weight. Potatoes do not make a person obese . . . it is foods containing sugar and white flour [that do]. In the United States, since 1900, potato consumption has gone down 60 per cent. Fats and oils have risen 50 per cent. Associated with these changes has been the development of all kinds of disease . . . (Poor nutrition is often held partly responsible for heart disease, kidney ailments and diabetes.)" —Fraser's Newsletter

Potato-Apple Muffins

Spicy light muffins, sure to be a favourite. Try the Blueberry-Orange variation.

½ cup raw potato, finely grated
1 cup apple, peeled and coarsely grated
⅔ cup whole wheat flour
1 cup all-purpose flour
¾ cup rolled oats
1 tbsp baking powder
½ tsp salt
¼ tsp nutmeg
¾ tsp cinnamon
1 cup brown sugar
1 egg, slightly beaten
¼ cup vegetable oil
1 cup milk

Grate potato and apple. Do not drain. Preheat oven to 400°F. Grease muffin tins. Measure flours, oatmeal, baking powder, salt, nutmeg, cinnamon and brown sugar into large mixing bowl; blend. Beat together egg, oil and milk. Add grated potato and apple. Stir into dry ingredients until mixture is thoroughly moistened. Do not overmix. Fill muffin tins three-quarters full and bake 15 to 20 minutes.
Makes 18 muffins.

Blueberry-Orange Muffin Variation: Decrease cinnamon to ½ teaspoon. Omit grated apple. Add grated rind of one orange and 1 cup fresh or frozen blueberries along with the dry ingredients. Mix and bake in similar manner to above recipe.

Potato Pineapple-and-Carrot Muffins

Light and delicious, hot or cold. These muffins are great for school lunch boxes.

1½ cups all-purpose flour
1 cup granulated sugar
2 tsp baking powder
1 tsp cinnamon
1 tsp baking soda
1 tsp salt

½ cup vegetable oil
2 eggs, lightly beaten
¾ cup finely grated carrot
¾ cup finely grated potato
¾ cup crushed pineapple (drain off about half the juice)

Preheat oven to 350°F. Lightly grease muffin tins. Combine flour, sugar, baking powder, cinnamon, baking soda and salt in large mixing bowl. Make a well in the centre of the mixture and add remaining ingredients. Mix lightly with a fork until just blended. Fill muffin tins two-thirds full. Bake 20 to 25 minutes.
Makes 24 muffins.

Spuds n' Spice Muffins

1½ cups very finely grated raw potato
2 tsp baking soda
1 cup whole wheat flour
½ cup all-purpose flour
3 tsp baking powder
½ tsp salt
¼ tsp nutmeg
¼ tsp ginger
¼ tsp mace
¾ cup brown sugar
⅓ cup currants
⅓ cup raisins
⅓ cup chopped walnuts
1 egg, slightly beaten
½ cup buttermilk
⅓ cup vegetable oil
½ tsp vanilla

Preheat oven to 400°F. Grease or line muffin cups. Grate potato into a large bowl, add soda and let stand until other ingredients are assembled. Measure and sift flours, baking powder, salt, nutmeg, ginger and mace. Add brown sugar, fruits and nuts. Combine buttermilk, egg, oil and vanilla. Beat well and stir into potato-soda mixture. Gradually add dry ingredients, mixing lightly just until blended. Fill muffin cups two-thirds full. Bake 20 minutes.
Makes 24 muffins.

Cinnamon-Potato Pinwheels

2 cups all-purpose flour
½ tsp salt
4 tsp baking powder
3 tbsp shortening
1 cup mashed potato
1 cup milk
1 tsp soft butter or margarine
¼ cup firmly packed brown sugar
1 tsp cinnamon

Preheat oven to 400°F. Combine flour, salt and baking powder. Cut in shortening until mixture resembles coarse meal. Add potato. Mix with milk to form a soft dough. Knead lightly. Roll to a 14x10-inch rectangle. Spread with soft butter. Mix brown sugar and cinnamon and spread over butter. Roll as a jelly roll. Seal edges. Slice in ½-inch slices and bake on a greased cookie sheet 12 to 15 minutes.
Makes 24 pinwheels.

Currant-Potato Scones

Quick to make, simple and delicious.

1¾ cups all-purpose flour
¼ cup granulated sugar
1 tbsp baking powder
1 tsp salt
⅓ cup butter, shortening or margarine
¾ cup mashed potato
¼ cup currants
⅓ cup milk
1 whole egg
1 egg yolk
1 egg white
granulated sugar

Preheat oven to 425°F. Combine flour, sugar, baking powder and salt. Cut in butter until mixture resembles coarse meal. Add potato. Mix lightly. Stir in currants. Mix together milk, whole egg and egg yolk. Stir with fork into dry ingredients until well-moistened. Turn dough onto a lightly floured board. Knead gently about 20 strokes. Roll into a circle with dough ½ inch thick. Brush with slightly beaten egg white

and sprinkle with sugar. Cut in 12 pie-shaped wedges and place on greased baking sheet. Bake 12 to 15 minutes.
Makes 12 scones.

English Potato Tea Scones

This recipe, served with strawberry jam, is a favourite for Sunday tea. It is an adaptation from the kitchen of Esmé Bromley of Derbyshire, England.

2 cups all-purpose flour
4 tsp baking powder
½ tsp salt
¼ cup granulated sugar
⅛ tsp nutmeg
½ cup margarine
¾ cup mashed potato
¾ cup raisins or currants
1 egg mixed with enough milk to make ⅔ cup

Preheat oven to 400°F. Combine dry ingredients. Cut in margarine. Thoroughly combine until mixture is crumbly. Add mashed potato and fruit. Toss lightly. Gently stir in egg-and-milk mixture using a fork. Mix only until blended. Knead lightly three or four times. Pat to one-inch thickness. Cut with a biscuit cutter or knife. Bake on a greased cookie sheet for 15 minutes.
Makes 24 scones.

Note: For a shiny golden top, I like to brush a bit of milk over the scones before baking.

The "Potato" in other languages

Arabic	*batata*
Dutch	*aardappel*
French	*pomme de terre*
German	*kartoffel*
Irish	*potato, pratie*
Italian	*patata*
Norwegian	*kartoffel*
Portuguese	*batata*
Spanish	*papa, patata*
Swedish	*potatis*
Swiss	*härdopfel*

Cheese-Potato Scones

These delicious cheese-topped scones come to us from Scotland.

⅓ cup shortening
1 cup hot mashed potato
1½ cups all-purpose flour
½ tsp salt
4 tsp baking powder
½ cup milk
1 egg, beaten
½ cup grated cheddar cheese

Preheat oven to 425°F. Melt shortening into hot mashed potato. Sift flour, salt and baking powder over potato mixture. Pour in milk, all at once. Mix just enough to moisten. Turn dough out onto a lightly floured board and knead 15 times. Roll out to ½-inch thickness and cut into triangles. Brush tops with beaten egg. Sprinkle with finely grated cheese. Bake on a lightly greased cookie sheet for 15 to 20 minutes. *Makes 18 scones.*

Yeast Breads

It is said that every cook since Cleopatra has at some time wanted to bake bread. No other culinary skill gives such personal satisfaction as the thrill of just-baked bread.

The early Egyptians were the first to discover a form of yeast. Since then, bread-making has had an important role in history. At one time the Greeks allowed only priests to make bread. The Romans turned bread-making over to the Civil Service. Bread has long been one of our most important and economical foods—as part of our heritage it is aptly called the "staff of life." Adding potatoes to bread dough makes for a moister loaf that keeps longer.

Bread-making is no longer the arduous all-day task our grandmothers knew. Today, quick-rising yeast and bread-kneading appliances have made bread-making a simple task.

The recipes here are written to be easily understood and followed to perfect results, even if you have never baked bread before. Read the recipes carefully and follow the basic rules and you will have beautiful bread every time.

"(The potato) . . . a fode, as also a meate for pleasure, . . . being either rosted in the embers, or boiled and eaten with oile, vinegar, and pepper, or dressed any other way by the hand of come cunning cookerie."—*John Berarde, 1597*

Hints for Making Better Bread

The water used to dissolve yeast should be about 105°F. To test the temperature, put a drop of water on the inside of your wrist. It should feel warm, but not hot. Water that is too hot will kill yeast action.

With the first addition of flour, beat the batter well to ensure that all ingredients are blended.

To knead dough, fold toward you and then push away with the heel of your hand. Rotate dough a quarter-turn and repeat until dough is smooth and surface looks blistered. A good way to tell if dough has been kneaded enough is to pinch the dough with one hand and at the same time squeeze your ear lobe. They will feel about the same.

Cover dough and set to rise in a warm, draft-free place.

To test for doubled bulk, stick fingertips into dough; the marks should remain if dough is doubled.

To punch down, shut your fist and plunge it into the centre of the dough.

Bake breads with the top of the pan level with the middle of the oven. Be sure pans have space all the way around them and are not touching the sides of the oven.

Bread is done when you tap the crust and it sounds hollow.

Remove bread from pans and place on wire racks to cool. Cool away from drafts.

Store bread in a tightly covered breadbox at room temperature, or wrap in foil or plastic wrap and put in your freezer. Bread dries out quickly if kept in the refrigerator.

Potato Bread

An economical bread that's extra special toasted. Freezes well.

1 cup lukewarm potato water
2 tsp sugar
2 tbsp yeast
2 cups scalded milk
1 cup mashed potato
2 tbsp sugar
2½ tsp salt
3 tbsp vegetable oil
8 to 8½ cups all-purpose flour

Combine potato water and sugar, stir well until sugar dissolves. Sprinkle with yeast and let stand 10 minutes. Meanwhile, scald milk and mix with mashed potato, sugar, salt and oil. Cool to lukewarm and add to yeast mixture. Add about half the flour and beat until smooth. Gradually mix the remaining flour to make a stiff dough. Turn onto a floured board and knead until smooth, about 8 minutes. Add extra flour if necessary. Place dough in a lightly greased bowl, turning the dough over to grease both sides. Cover with a towel and let rise until double in bulk. Punch down and turn onto a lightly floured board. Divide into four equal portions, cover and let rest for 10 to 15minutes. Shape into 4 loaves and place in greased 8x4-inch loaf pans. Cover and let rise until doubled, about 1 hour. Bake in preheated oven 350°F for 30 to 35 minutes. Cool on wire racks.
Makes 4 loaves.

The title of the world's oldest potato cookbook, written in 1664, is England's Happiness Increased . . . or a Sure and Easie Remedy against all succeeding Dear Years by A Plantation of the Roots called POTATOES, whereof (with the Addition of Wheat flour) excellent food and wholesome Bread may be made, every Year, eight or nine months together, for half the Charge as formerly. ALSO by the planting of these ROOTS, Ten thousand Men in England and Wales, who know not how to Live, or what to get Maintenance for their Families, may of One Acre of Ground, make Thirty Pounds per Annum, Invented and Published for the Good of the Poorer Sort by John Forster, Gent.

Potato Dough with Variations

This great recipe will yield a hundred rolls or doughnuts. It was given to me by Sue Carson of Indiana, U.S.

3 tbsp dry yeast
1 tsp granulated sugar
1 cup lukewarm water
4 cups scalded milk
2 cups mashed potato
1 cup margarine or butter
1 cup granulated sugar
18 cups all-purpose flour, divided
2 beaten eggs
1 tbsp salt

Dissolve 1 tsp sugar in lukewarm water. Sprinkle yeast over top and let sit for 10 minutes. Combine scalded milk, potato, margarine and sugar. Cool to lukewarm. Add yeast mixture and 6 cups flour. Mix well. Let stand until mixture foams (about 20 minutes). Add beaten eggs, salt and enough flour to make a stiff dough. Knead well. Put in a greased bowl and let rise until double in bulk. Punch down. Divide dough into 4 equal portions.

Doughnuts
Roll out to ¾-inch thickness. Cut with doughnut cutter. Place on trays and let rise until not quite doubled. Fry in hot oil (375°F). Drain on brown paper. Glaze while hot with the following mixture:

1 lb icing sugar
1 tbsp margarine
1 tsp vanilla
dash of mace
2 to 3 tbsp milk (to make a thin glaze)

Combine all ingredients and mix well.

Cinnamon Buns
Roll dough into a rectangle, about 18x9inches. Spread with butter. Sprinkle with a mixture of brown sugar and cinnamon. Roll like a jelly roll. Cut in 1½-inch slices. Place on greased pans. Cover and let rise until nearly doubled. Bake in preheated oven at 400°F for 15 to 20 minutes. Glaze with doughnut glaze.

Sticky Buns
Handle dough as for cinnamon buns. Grease pans heavily. Put a mixture of brown sugar, butter, corn syrup and cinnamon in bottom of pans. Put rolls on top. Let rise and bake as for cinnamon buns. Invert pan as soon as it is removed from the oven.

Dinner Rolls
Shape dough in desired ways. Place on greased pans. Let rise until nearly doubled. Bake in preheated oven at 400°F for 15 minutes. Brush tops with melted butter.

Coffee Cake
Put any scraps of remaining dough in a greased pan. Punch holes in dough with a spoon handle. Spread any leftover sugar, butter, syrup and cinnamon on top. Bake as for cinnamon buns. Use any leftover glaze to put on hot coffee cake.

All of these freeze well. Simply let cool and wrap in plastic.

Fluffy Potato Rolls

1 tbsp dry yeast
¼ cup lukewarm water
½ cup hot mashed potato
¼ cup shortening
¼ cup sugar
1½ tsp salt
1 cup scalded milk
1 egg
4 to 4½ cups all-purpose flour

Dissolve yeast in warm water. Combine potato, shortening, sugar, salt and hot milk. Cool to lukewarm. Add dissolved yeast and egg. Stir in flour to make a soft dough. Knead lightly on a floured surface until smooth and elastic (6 to 8 minutes). Place in a lightly greased bowl, turning over once to grease both sides. Cover. Let rise until double in bulk (about 1 hour). Punch down. Shape into a ball. Cover and let rest for 10 minutes. Shape into rolls. Place on a greased cookie sheet. Cover loosely and let rise until almost double in bulk (about 1 hour). Bake in a preheated 400°F oven for 10 to 12 minutes.
Makes 2 dozen rolls.

Southern Potato Bread

1 medium potato
¼ cup vegetable oil
¼ cup granulated sugar
1 tsp salt
1 tsp granulated sugar
1 tbsp dry yeast
¼ cup lukewarm water
1 egg
⅓ cup milk
3 to 3½ cups all-purpose flour
vegetable oil
melted butter

Peel potato, cut in chunks and boil until soft. Reserve water. Mash potato and add ½ cup potato water. Stir in vegetable oil, ¼ cup sugar and salt; mix well. Add remaining 1 tsp sugar and yeast to lukewarm water. Stir until dissolved. Set for 5 minutes until foamy. Add to potato mixture. Beat egg lightly and combine with milk. Add to potato mixture. In a large bowl, combine potato mixture and flour. Blend well to make a soft dough. Turn out on floured board and knead until smooth and elastic, about 10 minutes, using additional flour if necessary. Place in a greased bowl and turn dough over so both sides are greased. Cover tightly with plastic wrap and set in a warm place to rise until double in bulk. Punch down and knead lightly. Shape into a loaf and place in a greased 9x5-inch pan. Brush top with vegetable oil. Cover with plastic wrap and let rise until double in bulk. Preheat oven to 400°F. Bake loaf for 25 to 35 minutes until it sounds hollow when tapped. Turn out on wire rack to cool. Brush top with melted butter. Do not slice until completely cool.
Makes 1 loaf.

Potato Parkerhouse Rolls

Folding circles of dough in half makes the Parkerhouse Shape.

1 tbsp yeast
1 tsp granulated sugar
½ cup lukewarm water
1 cup mashed potato
7 cups all-purpose flour, divided
¾ cup shortening

½ cup granulated sugar
2 tsp salt
2 well-beaten eggs
1 cup scalded milk, cooled to lukewarm

Dissolve yeast and sugar in lukewarm water. Set aside for 10 minutes. Combine potato, 1 cup flour, shortening, sugar and salt. Add eggs and milk. Stir in yeast mixture. Cover and set in a warm place to rise for 2 hours. Add 6 cups of flour and knead well. Cover and let rise until double in bulk, about 1½ hours. Roll to ¼-inch thickness; cut with 2½-inch cookie cutter. Fold each roll over to form Parkerhouse shape. Let rise on a greased cookie sheet until double in bulk, about 1½ hours. Preheat oven to 425°F. Bake 30 to 35 minutes.
Makes 30 rolls.

Potato Refrigerator Rolls

The dough for this recipe can be prepared and stored for several days in the refrigerator before using.

1 cup warm mashed potato
1½ cups warm potato water or water
1 tbsp dry yeast
⅔ cup granulated sugar
1½ tsp salt
⅔ cup soft shortening
2 eggs, slightly beaten
7 to 7½ cups all-purpose flour

Cook potatoes; drain, reserving 1½ cups potato water. Dissolve yeast in potato water. Let stand 10 minutes. Add sugar, salt, shortening, eggs and mashed potato. Mix well. Add flour gradually and mix until smooth and elastic. Place in a greased bowl and turn over to grease the other side. Cover with a damp cloth and place in the refrigerator for at least 2 hours. Remove the desired amount of dough and shape into rolls. Cover and let rise until doubled, about 1½ to 2 hours. Bake for about 10 to 12 minutes in preheated 400°F oven.
Makes 4 dozen rolls.

"There is no species of human food that can be consumed in greater variety of modes than the potato."—*Sir John Sinclair, 1828*

Acadian Buns

An eighteenth-century recipe, I find these buns excellent for twentieth-century hamburgers.

2 cups water
2 medium potatoes
1 tbsp yeast
2 tsp sugar
½ cup water
7 to 7½ cups all-purpose flour
¾ cup lard*
2½ tsp salt
1 egg
2 tbsp sugar

Boil potatoes in water. Drain off ½ cup potato water. Set aside. Mash potatoes in remaining water. Let cool to lukewarm. Dissolve 2 tsp sugar in the ½ cup water and ½ cup reserved potato water (cooled to lukewarm). Sprinkle with 1 tbsp yeast. Let stand 10 minutes. Blend 6 cups flour, lard and salt. Beat egg and 2 tbsp sugar; add to yeast mixture. Gradually add dry ingredients. Mix well. Turn onto lightly floured board and knead until dough does not stick to hands, using extra flour if necessary. Let rise 1½ to 2 hours, until very light. Form into 36 buns. Place on three lightly greased cookie sheets, leaving space for spreading. Let rise until double in bulk, about 45 minutes. Bake in a preheated 400°F oven for 15 to 18 minutes.
Makes 36 buns.

* Be sure to use lard and **not** shortening in this recipe.

Even though some foods contain higher individual amounts of Vitamin C, potatoes, because of their greater popularity and consumption, rank second only to the total of all citrus fruits in the amount of Vitamin C contributed.

Canada's Food Guide recommends one serving of potato each day.

Chelsea Buns

A family favourite, these "sticky buns" are made as a special treat for birthday breakfasts.

½ cup lukewarm potato water
½ cup cooled mashed potato
1 tsp sugar
1 tbsp dry yeast
¼ cup butter or margarine, melted
¼ cup granulated sugar
2 eggs, well-beaten
½ tsp salt
3 cups all-purpose flour (approximate)
2 tbsp soft butter or margarine
¼ cup corn syrup
½ cup brown sugar
¼ tsp vanilla
½ cup coarsely chopped walnuts
2 tbsp soft butter or margarine
½ cup brown sugar
1½ tsp cinnamon
½ cup raisins

Combine potato water, mashed potato, sugar and yeast. Let stand in a warm place for 10 minutes. Add melted butter, granulated sugar and eggs. Beat well. Add salt and enough flour to make a soft dough. Knead on a lightly floured board until smooth and elastic. Place in a greased bowl. Turn over to lightly grease top of dough. Cover and let rise until double in bulk, about 1½ hours. Grease two 8-inch cake pans. Spread bottom of pans with mixture of soft butter, corn syrup, brown sugar, vanilla and walnuts. Roll dough into a 10x20-inch rectangle. Spread with soft butter and sprinkle with brown sugar, cinnamon and raisins. Roll as for jelly roll and cut into 32 even pieces. Place in pan. Cover and let rise about 1 hour. Bake in a preheated oven at 375°F for 10 minutes. Reduce heat to 350°F and bake another 15 to 20 minutes. Cool a few minutes and invert pan on waxed paper or a plate.
Makes 32 buns.

"To me they are glamorous, unique and special, an aristocrat among vegetables."—*James Beard, the famous chef, on potatoes*

Easy Hot Cross Buns

The flavours of nutmeg and citron make these old favourites just a bit different.

½ cup hot mashed potato
½ cup scalded milk
½ cup boiling potato water
⅓ cup margarine
⅓ cup granulated sugar
1 tsp salt
1 tsp finely grated orange rind
½ cup lukewarm water, or potato water
1 tsp granulated sugar
2 tbsp dry yeast
2 tsp cinnamon
½ tsp nutmeg
¼ tsp cloves
½ cup currants
½ cup raisins
½ cup citron peel
4 to 5 cups all-purpose flour
2 well-beaten eggs

Combine potato, milk, potato water, margarine, sugar, salt and orange rind. Stir until margarine melts. Cool to lukewarm. Meanwhile, dissolve 1 tsp sugar in lukewarm water. Sprinkle yeast over the top and let stand for 10 minutes. Combine spices, fruits and 2 cups flour. Beat into potato mixture. Add yeast and eggs. Blend well. Stir in enough additional flour to make a stiff dough. Knead well. Let rise until double in bulk, about 1½ hours. Form into 24 flat buns. Cut a cross on top of each bun with a sharp knife. Place on greased cookie sheets. Let rise until doubled. Bake in a preheated oven at 400°F for 15 to 18 minutes. Glaze while hot with doughnut glaze (see Doughnuts) if desired.
Makes 24 buns.

Several studies have shown that children consistently choose potatoes when asked to name their favourite vegetable.

Bagels

1 medium potato
2½ cups water
1 tbsp dry yeast
1½ tsp honey
1 tbsp vegetable oil
1 tbsp honey
1 whole egg
1 egg white (reserve yolk for glaze)
5 cups all-purpose flour (approximate)
3 qts water

Glaze
1 egg yolk
1 tsp cold water
poppy or sesame seeds

Boil sliced potato in 2½ cups water until soft. Drain, reserving water. Mash potato. Cool water to lukewarm. Start yeast in ½ cup potato water and 1½ tsp honey. To remaining potato water add oil, 1 tbsp honey, yeast mixture, mashed potato, egg, egg white and flour. When dough is stiff, knead for 8 to 10 minutes, adding extra flour if necessary. Place dough in a greased pan. Cover and let rise until almost double in bulk, about 45 minutes. Punch down and let rise again for 45 minutes. Shape dough into three 12-inch rolls. Cut each one into 8 equal pieces. Form each piece into a small roll. Moisten ends and form bagels. Let rise about 15 minutes. Meanwhile heat the 3 quarts of water to boiling. Reduce heat and simmer the bagels (afew at a time) for 5 minutes turning once. Drain and place on lightly oiled cookie sheets. Preheat oven to 425°F. Brush bagels with the glaze mixture and sprinkle with poppy or sesame seeds. Bake for 15 to 20 minutes. Cool on a wire rack. *Makes 24 bagels.*

"Always buy the best
Our spuds have good taste
And served properly
Won't go to your waist."   —*Sign in a potato display at a grocery store*

Sugar & Spice Loaf

This recipe makes six loaves of deliciously spicy bread. It is easy to make half the recipe; however, since Sugar & Spice Loaf freezes so well I always make the full amount.

1 cup mashed potato
2 cups boiling potato water or water
2½ cups milk, scalded
½ cup molasses
½ cup brown sugar
1 cup lard or shortening
3 tbsp dry yeast
3 tsp granulated sugar
½ cup lukewarm water
2 beaten eggs
6 cups whole wheat flour
3 tsp salt
3 tsp cinnamon
1 tsp nutmeg
1 tsp ginger
½ tsp cloves
2 cups raisins
6 to 8 cups all-purpose flour

Combine potato, boiling water, milk, molasses, brown sugar and lard. Mix well. Cool to lukewarm. Meanwhile, dissolve yeast and granulated sugar in lukewarm water. Let stand 10 minutes. Combine potato mixture and yeast. Add eggs, whole wheat flour, salt, spices and raisins. Beat well. Mix in enough all-purpose flour to make a stiff dough. Knead on a lightly floured board for 8 to 10 minutes, adding flour as needed to prevent sticking. Cover and let rise in a greased bowl for about 1½ hours. Shape into 6 loaves. Place in 8x4-inch greased loaf pans. Let rise 45 minutes. Bake in a preheated oven at 350°F for 50 minutes. *Makes 6 loaves.*

"The man who has not anything to boast of but his illustrious ancestors is like the potato—the only good thing belonging to him is underground."—*Sir Thomas Overbury, 1613*

Old-Fashioned Plum Loaf

From nineteenth-century Scotland, this recipe is sure to be a hit with everyone. It also freezes well.

2 cups scalded milk
1½ cups boiling potato water, or water
1 cup mashed potato
¾ cup brown sugar
½ cup shortening
½ cup lukewarm water
2 tbsp granulated sugar
2 tbsp dry yeast
8 cups all-purpose flour
2 tsp cinnamon
1 tsp nutmeg
2 tsp salt
1 tsp baking soda
2 cups seeded raisins
1 to 2 cups additional all-purpose flour

While milk is scalding, combine potato water, mashed potato, brown sugar and shortening. Add to milk. Cool to lukewarm. Meanwhile, dissolve 2 tbsp sugar in ½ cup lukewarm water. Sprinkle yeast over the top and let stand 10 minutes. Mix flour, cinnamon, nutmeg, salt and baking soda. Coat raisins in ¼ cup of this dry mixture. Combine yeast with potato mixture and add about half of the dry ingredients. Beat well. Stir in raisins and remaining dry ingredients to make a stiff dough. Knead 8 to 10 minutes, using additional flour if necessary. Cover and let rise 1½ hours. Form into 4 loaves. Let rise 1 hour. Bake in preheated 350°F oven for 50 to 60 minutes.
Makes 4 loaves.

Note: If using water instead of potato water, the rising time may be a few minutes longer.

Prince Edward Island is known as "Spud Island." This title is earned by the production of some of the finest seed and table potatoes grown in the world.

Spudnuts

A recipe from the kitchen of Isabel Campbell who writes, "It has become an established habit to make a batch of 'Spudnuts' several times during the winter, for the men in the warehouse grading potatoes. They look forward to 'Spudnut Day.' Besides being delicious, it breaks up their day."

1 tbsp dry yeast
1 tsp granulated sugar
¼ cup lukewarm water
2 cups scalded milk
½ cup butter or margarine
¾ tsp salt
3 well-beaten eggs
1 cup mashed potato
½ cup granulated sugar
6½ cups all-purpose flour (approximate)
oil for deep frying

Dissolve yeast and sugar in lukewarm water. Let stand 10 minutes. Scald milk and add butter and salt. Cool to lukewarm. Add eggs and blend well. Combine mashed potato and sugar; add milk mixture along with yeast. Mix well. Add enough all-purpose flour to make a soft dough. Let double in size in a warm place (about 3½ hours). Roll to ½-inch thickness. Cover and let rise until doubled. Heat oil for frying to 360°F. Snip small squares off the dough with scissors and quickly drop into hot oil. Brown on each side. Drain on rack. While hot, dip in glaze.
Makes 4 dozen

Spudnut Glaze

2 tbsp butter or margarine
2 tbsp hot milk
½ tsp vanilla
2 cups icing sugar (approximate)

Combine ingredients and mix to a spreading consistency.

An American football game held annually in Monte Vista, Colorado, is called "the Spud Bowl."

Fastnachts

Begin these special treats early in the day for a welcome homecoming to school children. Fastnachts come to us from Germany.

1 cup warm potato water
¾ cup granulated sugar
1 tsp salt
7 to 8 cups all-purpose flour
1 tsp granulated sugar
¼ cup lukewarm water
1 tbsp dry yeast
1 cup hot mashed potato
½ cup soft margarine or butter
¼ tsp nutmeg
fat for deep frying

Combine potato water, ¾ cup sugar, salt and 1 cup flour. Beat until smooth. Mix together 1 tsp sugar, lukewarm water and yeast. Stir to dissolve. Blend the two mixtures, cover and let stand in a warm place until bubbly (3 to 4 hours). Beat together hot mashed potato, margarine and nutmeg. Stir potato mixture into yeast mixture, adding enough flour to make a fairly stiff dough. Turn out on a lightly floured board and knead until smooth and elastic. Place in a greased bowl; cover and let rise in a warm place until double in bulk (1½ hours). Punch down and store in refrigerator until ready to use. Roll out to ⅓-inch thickness and cut with a doughnut cutter. Place on a floured board, cover and let rise another 1 to 1¼ hours. Heat fat to 365°F. Fry fastnachts (4 at a time) in hot fat. When they rise to the surface, turn them over. Fry until brown on both sides. Drain on absorbent paper. Dust with sugar. *Makes 3 to 4 dozen.*

Spicy Orange-Potato Doughnuts

5 to 5½ cups all-purpose flour
½ cup granulated sugar
1 tsp salt
1 tbsp grated orange rind
2 tbsp instant dry yeast*
1 cup lukewarm water
¼ cup margarine or butter
½ cup mashed potato
1 egg
oil for deep drying
1 cup granulated sugar
2 tsp cinnamon

Mix thoroughly 1½ cups of the flour, ½ cup sugar, salt, orange rind
and yeast. Heat the water and margarine to lukewarm and gradually
add to the dry ingredients. Beat 2 minutes. Add potato, egg and ½ cup
of the flour. Beat 2 minutes. Add remaining flour and stir to make a
soft dough. Turn onto a lightly floured board and knead until smooth
and elastic (about 8 to 10 minutes). Place in a greased bowl, turning
over to grease the top. Cover and allow to rise until double in bulk,
about 1 hour. Punch down, roll out to ½-inch thickness and cut with a
3-inch doughnut cutter. Place doughnuts on greased baking sheets.
Cover and let rise until double in bulk, about 30 minutes. Deep fry in
oil at 375°F until golden brown on both sides. Drain on absorbent paper.
Combine the remaining sugar and cinnamon, and dip doughnuts in
this mixture.
Makes about 36 doughnuts.

*If using regular yeast, dissolve in ½ cup lukewarm water before adding
to dry ingredients.

Irish Freckle Bread

A pioneer recipe with just a few big seeded raisins.

1 small potato
2 cups water
1 tsp granulated sugar
2 tbsp dry yeast
½ cup soft margarine or butter
½ cup granulated sugar

2 eggs, beaten
1 tsp salt
6 cups all-purpose flour (approximate)
1 cup seeded raisins

Boil potato in water until very tender. Drain, reserving water. Mash potato, set aside. Measure ½ cup potato water into a small bowl; cool to lukewarm. Add 1 tsp sugar; stir. Add yeast and let stand for 10 minutes. Meanwhile, combine remaining potato water, margarine and ½ cup sugar. Stir until margarine is melted. Add beaten eggs, salt and ¼ cup of the mashed potato. Stir in raisins and enough additional flour to make a soft dough. Knead on a lightly floured board until smooth and elastic. Place in a greased bowl. Lightly grease top of dough. Cover and let rise until double in bulk, about 1 hour. Punch down. Shape into 4 loaves. Put in greased 8-inch loaf pans. Cover and let rise until double in bulk, about 45 minutes. Bake in preheated oven at 350°F for 35 minutes.
Makes 4 loaves.

Golden Corn Bread

½ cup warm water
1 tsp sugar
1 tbsp dry yeast
1½ cups hot potato water
1 cup warm mashed potato
1 cup cornmeal
¼ cup corn syrup
¼ cup shortening
2 tsp salt
4 cups all-purpose flour

Combine warm water, sugar and yeast; let stand 10 minutes. Combine potato water, mashed potato, cornmeal, corn syrup, shortening and salt. Let stand until yeast mixture is ready. Add yeast mixture to potato mixture along with 2 cups flour. Beat well. Stir in enough additional flour to make a stiff dough. Knead on a lightly floured board, adding more flour if necessary. Let rest 15 minutes. Shape into 2 loaves. Place in greased 8x4-inch loaf pans. Cover and let rise until dough reaches top of pans. Bake in preheated 400°F oven for 15 minutes, then reduce heat to 350°F and bake for 25 minutes. If desired, brush tops of loaves with melted butter after removing from oven.
Makes 2 small loaves.

Frosted Fruit Ring

Our daughter Marina was eight years old when she adapted this recipe from a magazine. Frosted Fruit Ring, alias "Marina's Christmas Bread," has become a tradition at our house.

1¼ cups cream of potato soup (one 10 oz can)
¾ cup potato water
½ cup margarine or butter
3 cups all-purpose flour
2 tbsp instant dry yeast
½ tsp salt
3 tbsp granulated sugar
3 eggs, well-beaten
½ cup candied mixed fruit
½ cup golden raisins
½ cup candied cherries, quartered
3 to 3½ cups all-purpose flour

Combine soup, water and margarine in a saucepan. Heat over medium heat until margarine is melted and mixture is lukewarm. Pour into a large mixing bowl. Combine flour, yeast, salt and sugar. Add to potato mixture. Stir in eggs and beat at medium speed for 3 to 4 minutes until well-blended. Stir in by hand fruit and enough flour to make a stiff dough. Knead on a lightly floured board, using additional flour as required until dough is smooth and satiny and does not stick to your hands. Place in a greased bowl, turning over once to grease both sides. Cover and let rise until double in bulk, about 1 hour. Roll half the dough into a 24x6-inch rectangle. Cut into 3 lengthwise strips. Form the strips into a braid and place in two greased 10-inch tubepans. Cover and let rise until doubled, about 1 hour. Bake in a preheated oven at 375°F for 20 to 25 minutes. Glaze with a confectioner's glaze if desired. *Makes 2 rings.*

*If potato soup is lumpy, sieve or whirl in blender.

One of the first planting and harvesting tools used in growing potatoes was a hoe-type instrument called a "spud." When harvesting potatoes, one would go "spudding." Many people say the nickname "spud" came from the ancient farm implement.

Honey Whole Wheat Bread

Delicious warm from the oven with home-bakes beans.

4 cups whole wheat flour
½ cup dry milk powder
2 tbsp yeast
1 tbsp salt
2½ cups potato water
½ cup honey
2 tbsp oil
4 cup white all-purpose flour (more if necessary)

Dissolve 1 tsp sugar in ½ cup warm water, and mix 3 cups whole wheat flour, dry milk powder, yeast and salt in a large bowl. Heat the potato water, honey and oil until warm, about 120–130°F. Pour over flour mixture. Beat with electric mixer 3 minutes. Stir in remaining cup of whole wheat flour and white flour. Knead 5 minutes using additional flour if necessary. Let rise in greased bowl until double in bulk, about 1½ hours. Punch down and divide in half. Form two loaves. Place in greased 9x5-inch loaf pans. Cover let rise 40 to 45 minutes. Bake in 375°F oven for 40 to 45 minutes.
Makes 2 large loaves.

Variation: Add ¼ cup wheat germ

Potato-Water Sourdough

No potato cookbook would be complete without a recipe for sourdough. One of the first baking products made with potatoes was potato yeast or potato sourdough. Used before the invention of baking powder, the first recipes were made with hops. Today we use regular dry yeast with equally satisfying results.

Early pioneers depended on sourdough as their main leavening agent. Today it is used as an enhancer to baked goods, giving a lighter texture and superior taste. There are many variations of sourdough starter. I have included my favourite. Sourdough can be made using raw potato, mashed potato or simply potato water. It can be used again and again by simply measuring out the required amount for your recipe and "feeding" the remaining starter with equal amounts of all-purpose flour and lukewarm water, at least once a week. Let starter sit at room temperature for 12 hours after feeding. If a clear liquid appears on top of your starter, simply stir.

Keep a supply of sourdough starter on hand. There's no end to possibilities for its use.

2½ cups potato water, lukewarm (be sure water is not too hot)
1¾ cups all-purpose flour
1 tbsp salt
1 tbsp granulated sugar
1 tbsp dry yeast

In a medium bowl combine flour, salt, sugar and yeast. Mix well. Stir in potato water. Cover with a towel and set in a warm place, free from drafts, for 48 hours. Mixture will become bubbly. Stir the mixture several times a day. Store in refrigerator in glass or plastic container with a hole punched in the cover. "Feed" your sourdough once a week with 1 cup flour and 1 cup lukewarm water. I remove my starter from the refrigerator the night before I want to use it. I measure out the amount I will use, feed the remainder and leave it out overnight before returning it to the refrigerator.

Cheese-and-Potato Sourdough Bread

Two loaves of an old-country classic.

2 tbsp dry yeast
½ cup lukewarm water
1 tsp sugar
1 cup sourdough starter
2 cups lukewarm potato water or water
1½ cups grated cheddar cheese
½ tsp baking powder
2 tbsp vegetable oil
2 tbsp granulated sugar
2 tbsp salt
2 cups mashed potato
7 cups all-purpose flour (approximate)

Combine yeast, water and sugar. Let stand 10 minutes. Mix remaining ingredients together (except flour). Mix well. Add dissolved yeast and gradually add flour. Stir well after each addition. Add enough flour to make a firm dough. Knead on a lightly floured surface until smooth and elastic, using additional flour if necessary. Lightly grease dough. Place in a warm bowl; cover and set in a draft-free place to rise until doubled. Punch down, form into loaves. Let rise 2 hours in greased loaf pans. Preheat oven to 375°F and bake 45 minutes.
Makes 2 loaves.

Thomas Jefferson is credited with having introduced French fries into the White House, sometime in 1801.

"Every country seems to top its French fries differently. The French serve them crisp and brown with salt and pepper; the Dutch and Belgians in small paper cones with a dollop of mustard and mayonnaise; the English serve fries with vinegar; the Spanish with pepper only; and all of North America love to pour on the ketchup."—U.S Potato Board

Cookies

The first time your children raid the cupboards, chances are they will be looking for cookies. Soon they'll want to bake them too! Milk and cookies have welcomed the new kid on the block, helped heal scraped knees and sealed friendship pacts for children over the decades. Equally good in lunch boxes, at picnics, on a hike or for a T.V. or late-night snack, cookies symbolize a friendly home.

Double-Chocolate Potato Cookies

½ cup shortening
1 cup brown sugar, firmly packed
1 egg
1 tsp vanilla
2 squares unsweetened chocolate, melted
½ cup mashed potato (room temperature)
1½ cups all-purpose flour
½ tsp salt
½ tsp baking soda
¾ cup sour milk
½ cup chopped nuts

Preheat oven to 400°F. Cream together shortening and brown sugar until light and fluffy. Beat in egg and vanilla, mixing well. Add chocolate and mashed potato and beat until smooth. Sift together flour, salt and baking soda. Add alternately with sour milk to creamed mixture. Stir until smooth. Add nuts. Drop by rounded teaspoons on a greased baking sheet. Bake about 10 minutes or until they spring back when touched. Do not overbake. Cool slightly.
Makes 40 cookies.

Frosting
1 tbsp soft butter or margarine
1 square unsweetened chocolate, melted
1½ tbsp warm water
1 cup icing sugar, sifted

Combine ingredients; mix well. Spread over cookies.

Coconut-Crunch Cookies

1 cup soft shortening
1 cup brown sugar
1 cup granulated sugar
2 eggs, slightly beaten
1 tsp almond extract
1 tsp vanilla
1½ cups all-purpose flour
1 tsp baking soda
1 tsp baking powder
¼ tsp salt
¼ tsp cloves
½ tsp nutmeg
2 cups shredded coconut
1 cup crushed potato chips
2 cups rolled oats

Preheat oven to 375°F. Combine shortening, sugars and eggs in a large mixing bowl. Beat until light and fluffy. Stir in almond and vanilla flavourings. Sift flour, baking soda, baking powder, salt, cloves and nutmeg. Blend into creamed mixture. Stir in coconut, potato chips and rolled oats. Roll in small balls. Place on a greased cookie sheet. Flatten with a fork. Bake 12 to 15 minutes. These cookies will become crisp as they cool.
Makes 6 dozen.

Holiday Hermits

A holiday recipe that you will want to use all year round.

1 cup soft shortening or margarine
2 cups brown sugar, firmly packed
2 large eggs
1 cup mashed potato
½ cup potato water
3 cups all-purpose flour
1 tsp salt
1 tsp baking soda
1 tsp nutmeg
1 tsp cinnamon
1 tsp instant coffee
1 cup chopped walnuts
1 cup seedless raisins or chopped dates

Preheat oven to 400°F. Cream shortening and sugar. Add eggs, potato
and potato water; beat well. Sift together flour, salt, baking soda, nutmeg and cinnamon. Add to creamed mixture. Stir in coffee, nuts and
raisins. Chill at least one hour. Drop by teaspoons on greased cookie
sheet. Bake 9 to 10 minutes.
Makes 6 dozen cookies.

P.E.I. Drop Cookies

⅔ cup butter or margarine
1 cup brown sugar
1 egg, slightly beaten
2 tsp vanilla
2 tsp grated orange rind
1 cup grated carrot
½ cup mashed potato
1½ cups all-purpose flour
1½ tsp baking powder
¼ tsp salt

Preheat oven to 400°F. Cream butter and brown sugar. Add egg and
vanilla and mix well. Beat in orange rind, carrot and potato. Sift together flour, baking powder and salt; add to the potato mixture. Drop
by teaspoons onto a cookie sheet. Bake 10 to 12 minutes.
Makes 40 cookies.

Doodle Drops

Delicious fresh from the oven, especially with cold milk. This recipe is an adaptation of the Danish favourite, Snickerdoodles.

½ cup shortening
½ cup butter or margarine
1½ cups granulated sugar
2 eggs
½ cup mashed potato
2¾ cups all-purpose flour
2 tsp cream of tartar
¼ tsp salt
1 tsp baking soda
2 tbsp granulated sugar
2 tsp cinnamon

Cream shortening and butter. Add sugar and blend well. Beat in eggs. Add potato, flour, cream of tartar, salt and baking soda. Mix well. Chill until easy to handle. Preheat oven to 400°F. Roll dough in walnut-sized balls. Roll in a mixture of cinnamon and sugar. Bake 8 to 10 minutes. Cookies will feel soft on top but will firm up when cooled.
Makes 4 dozen 2½-inch cookies.

Oatmeal Cookies

1 cup all-purpose flour
1 cup quick cooking rolled oats
½ tsp salt
½ tsp cinnamon
¼ tsp baking soda
½ cup mashed potato
2 tbsp potato water or water
¾ cup butter or margarine
¾ cup brown sugar
¼ cup granulated sugar
1 egg, beaten
1 tsp vanilla
½ cup chopped nuts
½ cup raisins

Preheat oven to 350°F. Combine flour, oats, salt, cinnamon and baking soda. Set aside. Beat potato and water together until no lumps remain. Cream butter, sugars and egg until light. Add vanilla. Add potato mixture and blend until well-mixed. Stir in dry ingredients until batter is smooth. Fold in nuts and raisins. Drop on lightly greased cookie sheet. Bake 15 to 20 minutes or until golden brown.
Makes 4 dozen cookies.

Surprise Cookies

1½ cups all-purpose flour
1½ tsp baking powder
¼ tsp salt
⅔ cup butter or margarine
1 cup brown sugar
1 egg
2 tsp vanilla
½ cup mashed potato
½ cup nuts
2 tsp orange rind
1 cup grated raw carrot
½ cup raisins

Preheat oven to 400°F. Combine flour, baking powder and salt. Set aside. Cream butter, sugar and egg until light. Add vanilla. Add potato and beat until no lumps remain. Blend in dry ingredients and mix

until smooth. Fold in nuts, orange rind, carrot and raisins. Drop by teaspoons onto an ungreased cookie sheet. Bake 10 to 12 minutes or until golden brown.
Makes 4 dozen.

Sourdough Drop Cookies

1 cup shortening
2 cups firmly packed brown sugar
2 eggs
¾ cup Potato Sourdough (see Yeast Breads)
¾ cup mashed potato
2¼ cups all-purpose flour
1 tsp salt
1 tsp baking soda
1 cup raisins
1 tsp vanilla

Preheat oven to 350°F. Cream shortening and sugar; add eggs, sourdough and mashed potato. Sift flour, salt and soda and add to mixture. Stir in raisins and vanilla. Drop on greased cookie sheets and bake 10 to 12 minutes.
Makes 4 dozen cookies.

Variations: Chopped nuts, chocolate chips, coconut or cherries may be substituted for the raisins.

Potato-Peanut Crunchies

If using salted peanuts in this recipe, omit the extra salt.

½ cup butter or margarine
¼ cup peanut butter
½ cup mashed potato (slightly warmed)
½ cup brown sugar
½ cup granulated sugar
1 egg
2 cups all-purpose flour
¼ tsp salt
½ tsp baking soda
½ tsp cinnamon
⅛ tsp cloves
½ cup finely chopped peanuts

Preheat oven to 400°F. Cream butter, peanut butter and potato. Gradually blend in sugars and beat with electric mixer until light. Add egg and beat one minute longer. Combine dry ingredients; add to batter. Fold in chopped peanuts. Drop by teaspoons on ungreased cookie sheet and bake 10 to 12 minutes.
Note: These cookies can be shaped in rolls, refrigerated, sliced and baked when desired (dough will keep up to a week).
Makes 4 dozen cookies.

Potato-Cranberry-Apple Drop Cookies

1 cup grated raw potato (use fine blade on grater)
1 cup chopped cranberries
1 cup apple, peeled and chopped or grated finely
1½ tsp grated orange rind
½ cup butter or margarine
1 cup brown sugar
¾ cup granulated sugar
1 egg
¼ cup milk
2 cups all-purpose flour
1 tsp baking powder
1 tsp cinnamon
½ tsp salt

Preheat oven to 375°F. Prepare potatoes, cranberries, apple and orange rind. Cream butter and sugars; beat in egg and milk. Sift flour, baking powder, cinnamon and salt. Stir into butter mixture until well-blended. Stir in orange rind, potato, apple and cranberries. Drop by teaspoons onto greased cookie sheets. Bake 12 to 15 minutes.
Makes 4 dozen cookies.

Potato-Chips Cookies

A recipe from the potato chip capital of the world: the United States. You will make these scrumptious cookies again and again. You may want to omit the extra salt if you use salted potato chips.

1 cup brown sugar
1 cup granulated sugar
1 cup shortening
2 eggs
1 tsp vanilla
2 cups crushed potato chips
2 cups oatmeal
2 cups all-purpose flour
1 tsp salt
1 tsp baking soda

Preheat oven to 375°F. Cream sugars and shortening. Beat in eggs and vanilla. Add remaining ingredients and mix well. Drop by teaspoons on a baking sheet. Bake 10 to 15 minutes.
Makes 6 dozen cookies.

"... a rascally heap of sand and swamp ... in the horrible Gulf of St. Lawrence ... That lump of worthlessness bears nothing but potatoes." — *William Cobbet in his book,* The English Gardener, *writing about Prince Edward Island*

"Be eating one potato, peeling a second, have a third in your fist and your eye on a fourth." — *Old Irish saying*

Potato Leatherbacks

Adapted from a recipe my mother made for lunch boxes when I was in school. Don't let the name fool you: these cookies are *not* leathery!

½ cup molasses
½ cup butter or margarine
⅓ cup brown sugar
1½ cups mashed potato
2 cups all-purpose flour
½ tsp baking soda
½ tsp ginger
1 tsp cinnamon
½ tsp salt
2 tsp baking powder
1 cup raisins
granulated sugar (optional)

Preheat oven to 375°F. Heat molasses and butter until butter melts. Add sugar; blend well. Stir in mashed potato. Sift dry ingredients. Stir raisins into dry ingredients and add to creamed mixture. Form dough in walnut-sized balls. Roll in granulated sugar. Bake on greased cookie sheet for 10 minutes.
Makes 4 dozen cookies.

Cherry Pecan Snowballs

½ cup soft butter or margarine
½ cup icing sugar
¼ cup cold mashed potato
2 tbsp milk
1 tsp almond flavouring
¼ tsp salt
1¾ cups all-purpose flour
½ cup chopped pecans
maraschino cherries, drained and halved
additional icing sugar

Preheat oven to 325°F. Cream butter and icing sugar. Blend in potato, milk, flavouring and salt. Stir in flour and pecans. Mix well. Form dough in small balls with half a cherry inserted in the centre. Bake on greased cookie sheet for 15 to 18 minutes. Cool slightly and roll in icing sugar.
Makes 40 cookies.

Sugared Potato-Cakes

The origin of this recipe is unknown. It was previously published using vanilla sugar instead of vanilla in the CIP Women's Club Cookbook from Peru.

5 tbsp butter or margarine
1 tbsp granulated sugar
1 tsp vanilla
3 egg yolks
4 to 5 tbsp sour cream
1 lb potatoes (3 medium), cooked, peeled and finely grated, approx. 2 cups
2 cups sifted all-purpose flour
3 egg whites
apricot or raspberry jam
butter or margarine
3 tbsp granulated sugar
1 tbsp cinnamon

Cream together butter, sugar, vanilla and egg yolks. Fold in sour cream. Into this, mix potato and flour. Quickly mix together to form a supple dough. Roll out to scarcely ½-inch thickness. Cut in 3-inch circles (be sure to have an even number of circles). Brush the edges of half the circles with egg white. Fill the centre with thick jam. Cover with remaining rounds and press the edges together delicately. Brown on each side in butter in frying pan. Mix sugar and cinnamon. Roll cakes in cinnamon sugar while still warm.
Makes 4 to 5 dozen cookies.

Potatoes provide, per unit of land, more calories and more protein than any other major food crop—five times as much food as corn, wheat or soybeans.

It takes twenty-three medium potatoes to make up 2500 calories, the daily required calories of an average adult. On top of his regular diet, a person would have to eat eleven pounds of potatoes to put on one pound of weight.

Cherry-Pecan Chews

1 cup all-purpose flour
1 cup brown sugar, firmly packed
½ cup cold mashed potato
1 cup rolled oats
1 tsp baking soda
¼ tsp salt
½ cup butter or margarine
2 eggs, beaten
1 cup brown sugar, lightly packed
½ tsp almond flavouring
2 tbsp all-purpose flour
½ tsp salt
1 cup coconut
1 cup well-drained maraschino cherries, halved
½ cup pecans, halved

Preheat oven to 350°F. Combine flour, 1 cup brown sugar, potato, rolled oats, baking soda, salt and butter. Mix with a pastry blender until crumbly. Press in the bottom of a 13x9x2-inch cake pan. Bake 10 minutes. Remove from oven. Meanwhile, combine remaining ingredients, except for the pecans. Stir until well-blended and pour over cooked portion. Sprinkle pecan halves on top. Return to oven and bake for an additional 25 minutes. Cool thoroughly.

Frosting
¼ cup butter or margarine
2 cups icing sugar
¼ tsp almond extract
2 tbsp maraschino cherry juice (approximate)

Blend butter and sugar; add flavouring and enough cherry juice to make a spreading consistency.

Cranberry Christmas Squares

⅔ cup shortening
⅔ cup warm mashed potato
⅔ cup icing sugar
1 tsp vanilla
2 egg yolks
1¾ cups all-purpose flour

Topping
1 whole egg
2 egg whites
1 cup granulated sugar
⅓ cup all-purpose flour
¼ tsp salt
1 tsp baking powder
1 tsp almond flavouring
⅓ cup raisins
⅓ cup chopped almonds
½ cup coconut
⅔ cup cranberry sauce

Preheat oven to 350°F. Cream shortening, potato and icing sugar. Add vanilla and egg yolks and mix well. Stir in flour. Spread on a greased 9-inch square cake pan. Beat whole egg and egg whites until light. Add granulated sugar and continue beating until mixture resembles whipped cream. Fold in remaining ingredients, blending well. Pour over unbaked crust. Bake 40 to 45 minutes. Cool in pan. Ice with lemon-flavoured icing.

The largest potato grown in Britain to date weighed 7 pounds, 1 ounce. It was grown by J.H. East of Spalding in 1963.

Chocolate-Walnut Potato Squares

I like to top these squares with small dollops of butter icing and pieces of chopped walnuts. Attractive and tasty for special occasions.

Base:
⅓ cup shortening
⅓ cup warm mashed potato
⅓ cup icing sugar
½ tsp vanilla
1 egg yolk
1 cup flour

Topping:
1 egg white
1 whole egg
1 cup brown sugar
1 tbsp flour
½ tsp baking powder
¼ tsp salt
1½ tbsp cocoa
½ cup finely grated walnuts

Preheat oven to 375°F. Combine shortening, potato, icing sugar, vanilla and egg yolk. Mix until creamy and well-blended. Stir in flour. Pat into an 8-inch square cake pan. Bake 10 minutes. Remove from oven. Reduce oven heat to 350 Prepare topping by beating egg white and whole egg until light and fluffy. Combine dry ingredients. (If cocoa is lumpy put it through a sieve.) Stir dry ingredients and walnuts into eggs. Spread over cooked base. Return to oven and bake 30 minutes. When cool, ice and decorate if disired.

Variations: the base for these squares can be used for several variations of bar cookies. I particularly like to use this when baking for Christmas. I simply multiply the base recipe by the number of pans of squares I want to make and then use a variety of toppings.

Fruit-and-Vegetable-Fudge Squares

Moist and tender squares with a creamy fudge icing.

1 cup raisins
1 tsp baking soda
1 cup boiling potato water
¼ cup shortening
1 cup granulated sugar
2 cups all-purpose flour
2 tsp baking powder
¼ tsp salt
1 tsp vanilla
½ cup finely grated carrot
½ cup finely grated potato

Pour boiling water over raisins and baking soda. Cool to lukewarm. Preheat oven to 350°F. Grease and flour a 9x13-inch cake pan. Cream shortening; add sugar and raisin mixture. Sift dry ingredients. Add to creamed mixture along with vanilla and grated vegetables. Mix well. Spread in prepared pan and bake 30 minutes. Cool thoroughly.

Fudge Icing
3 tbsp butter or margarine
3 tbsp brown sugar
2 tbsp cream or evaporated milk
1 tsp vanilla or desired flavouring
icing sugar

Heat butter, sugar and cream until butter and sugar are melted. Add vanilla or desired flavouring and enough icing sugar to make a spreading consistency. Spread on cool cake. Decorate with walnuts if desired.

"The potato is the world's greatest plant." — *W.F. Wright, 1917*

California Potato-Date Squares

1 medium potato, peeled and boiled in 1¼ cups water
1 cup chopped dates
1 tsp baking soda
¼ cup shortening
1 cup granulated sugar
1 egg
1 tsp vanilla
1¾ cups flour
¼ tsp salt

Topping:
4 tbsp melted butter or margarine
4 tbsp cream or evaporate milk
½ cup brown sugar
1 cup coconut
1 tsp vanilla

Drain water from cooked potato and reserve 1 cup to pour over dates. Let dates, potato water and baking soda sit until they cool to room temperature. Mash potato; cool to room temperature. Preheat oven to 350°F. Grease and lightly flour a 9x13-inch cake pan. Cream shortening; add sugar and egg. Beat well. Stir in vanilla and mashed potatoes. Add flour and salt alternately with date and water mixture. Mix well. Bake in prepared pan for 30 minutes. Meanwhile combine topping ingredients. When cake is finished baking, remove from oven and spread topping over cake. Return to oven and bake until brown or put under the broiler for 3 to 4 minutes.

Nutritionists agree that the diet of nineteenth century Ireland, five pounds of potatoes and one quart of milk per day, provided all nutrients essential to a human being.

Butterscotch Congo Bars

⅔ cup soft shortening or margarine
⅔ cup warm mashed potato
2 cups brown sugar
1 tsp vanilla
3 eggs
¼ tsp salt
1½ tsp baking powder
1¾ cups all-purpose flour
2 cups butterscotch chips

Preheat oven to 350°F. Grease a 9x13-inch cake pan and line with waxed paper. Cream shortening and potato. Add brown sugar and blend until light. Beat in vanilla and eggs. Sift salt, baking powder and flour; stir into other mixture. Spread in prepared pan. Sprinkle with butterscotch chips, pressing them lightly into batter with back of a spoon. Bake 25 to 30 minutes.

Cherry-Almond Bars

Prepare and cook base (see page 102). Top with the following:

1 egg white
1 whole egg
1 cup brown sugar
½ tsp almond flavouring
½ tsp baking powder
1 tbsp all-purpose flour
½ cup finely chopped blanched almonds
½ cup finely chopped candied cherries

Beat egg white and whole egg. Add sugar and flavouring; mix well. Stir in remaining ingredients. Pour over cooked base. Return to oven and bake 30 minutes. Frost with butter icing.

Potato Maple-Walnut Dream Bars

Rich and delicious!

⅓ cup shortening
⅓ cup warm mashed potato
⅓ cup icing sugar
½ tsp vanilla
1 egg yolk
1 cup all-purpose flour

Topping
½ cup brown sugar
½ cup Potato Maple Syrup (see Miscellaneous)
2 eggs, beaten
1 tbsp all-purpose flour
½ tsp baking powder
¼ tsp salt
½ tsp vanilla
½ cup coconut
1 cup grated walnuts

Preheat oven to 400°F. Beat shortening, potato and icing sugar until well-blended. Add vanilla and egg yolk. Mix well. Stir in flour. Pat into a greased 8-inch square cake pan. Bake 10 minutes. Remove from oven. Reduce oven heat to 350°F. Combine brown sugar, maple syrup and beaten eggs. Beat until light and creamy. Add remaining ingredients. Mix until well-blended. Pour over slightly cooled base. Return to oven and bake 20 to 25 minutes. Cool in pan. May be frosted when cool with butter icing.

Coffee-Nut Potato Bars

1 medium potato, peeled and cubed
⅔ cup potato water
1 tbsp instant coffee
½ cup butter or margarine
2 cups brown sugar
2 eggs
1 tsp vanilla
2 cups all-purpose flour
1 tsp salt
2 tsp baking powder

Boil potato until tender. Drain, reserving cooking water. Mash potato and cool slightly. Combine ⅔ cup of cooking water with instant coffee; set aside. Preheat oven to 350°F. Grease a 9x13-inch cake pan and line bottom with waxed paper. Cream butter, potato and brown sugar. Add eggs and beat until light and fluffy. Sift and stir in dry ingredients alternately with ½ cup coffee mixture. Save remaining coffee for frosting. Spread in prepared pan and bake for 30 to 35 minutes.

Frosting
2 tbsp butter or margarine
2 cups icing sugar
1 tbsp cocoa
1 tsp vanilla
reserved coffee, about 2 to 3 tbsp

Combine butter, icing sugar, cocoa, vanilla and enough coffee to make a spreading consistency. Spread over cooled squares.

Pioneer children brought their potatoes to school and gave them to the caretaker or the teacher. He would carve each child's initials in their "tater" and put them on the stove. At recess the children would have a tasty, healthy snack.

Cakes

I have always associated cakes with happiness. Traditionally cakes were served for company on special occasions—Christmas, Easter, birthdays, weddings, christenings or when Grandma came to visit. There's a cake for everyone and for every occasion. World leaders and celebrities have cakes named for them—Queen Elizabeth Cake, Lord and Lady Baltimore Cakes, to name a few.

For a special day, or just because you feel good, why not make someone happy by baking a cake.

Note: remember when baking cakes to grease the bottom of the pans, but not the sides. Your cake will have a smooth level top. It is not easy to climb a greased pan. (Also, when recipe calls for mashed potatoes be sure they are very finely mashed or riced—you don't want any lumps!)

The potato industry in Canada dates back to 1623 when a small patch was grown at Port Royal, Nova Scotia.

"A diet that consists predominantly of rice leads to the use of opium, just as a diet which consists predominantly of potatoes leads to the use of liquor."—*F.W. Nietzsche*

Boiled Raisin Cake

During the Second World War, when fruit and nuts were not available, this recipe was used to make an economical fruit cake. I like to add a few candied cherries and mixed fruit and use this recipe for my Dark Fruit Cake each Christmas. It is not nearly as rich as the traditional fruit cake and can be made almost at the last minute.

2 cups boiling potato water
2 cups granulated sugar
½ cup butter or margarine
½ cup lard
2 cups raisins
2 tsp cinnamon
1 tsp cloves
1 tsp salt
2 tsp baking soda
3½ cups all-purpose flour
2 tsp baking powder
½ cup finely mashed potato

Grease and line a 10-inch tube pan with 2 layers of waxed paper or 1 layer of brown paper that has been greased on the inside. In a medium saucepan combine potato water, sugar, butter, lard, raisins, cinnamon, cloves and salt. Bring to a boil and simmer 1 minute. Remove from heat; add 2 tsp baking soda and cool to room temperature. Preheat oven to 350°F. Add remaining ingredients. Blend well. Pour into prepared pan. Bake for approximately 1½ hours. A small container of water in the oven will make a moister cake.

Fruit-Cake Variation: Add 2 to 3 cups candied citron, cherries or mixed fruit to the first mixture before boiling.

Chocolate Potato Layer Cake

½ cup milk
½ cup plus 2 level tbsp cocoa
1 cup plus 1½ tbsp butter or margarine
1¾ cups granulated sugar
1 cup hot mashed potato
4 egg yolks
2 cups sifted all-purpose flour
1 tbsp baking powder
¼ tsp salt
1 tsp vanilla
4 egg whites
¼ cup granulated sugar

Preheat oven to 350°F. Grease and flour three 8-inch cake pans. Heat milk slowly in a saucepan. Add cocoa and 1½ tbsp butter. Stir until melted and mix well. Cool. Cream remaining butter with 1¾ cups sugar until light and fluffy. Combine chocolate mixture with potato and add to creamed mixture. Beat in egg yolks. Sift together flour, baking powder and salt; stir into batter. Add vanilla. Beat egg whites until stiff, adding the ¼ cup sugar gradually. Fold into batter. Pour into prepared pans. Bake for 30 minutes. Cool on racks and frost as desired or sprinkle with icing sugar.

Cherry Chocolate Cake

½ cup shortening
⅔ cup mashed potato
1½ cups granulated sugar
3 eggs
2 squares unsweetened chocolate, melted over hot water
2 cups all-purpose flour
1½ tsp baking soda
¾ tsp baking powder
¾ tsp salt
1¼ cups sour milk or buttermilk
¼ cup maraschino cherry juice
⅓ cup maraschino cherries, drained and halved

Preheat oven to 375°F. Grease and flour two 9-inch cake pans. Cream together shortening, potato and sugar. Add eggs, one at a time, beating well after each addition. Stir in melted chocolate. Sift flour, baking soda, baking powder and salt at least twice. Stir cherry juice into sour milk. Add dry ingredients to batter alternating with milk mixture, making several additions, beginning and ending with dry ingredients. Stir in cherries. Bake in prepared pans for 35 minutes. Cool on racks. Frost with Butter Cream Icing flavoured with almond or cherry.

Butter Cream Icing
3 tbsp soft butter or margarine
pinch salt
½ tsp vanilla, lemon or almond flavouring
2 cups icing sugar
2 to 2½ tsp warm milk

Cream butter; add salt and flavouring. Blend in icing sugar alternately with milk. Beat until smooth. For a layer cake, use a double recipe.

Easy Black Forest Cake

This cake also makes a delicious plain chocolate cake when iced with any desired frosting.

3 squares unsweetened chocolate
½ cup butter or margarine (soften but do not melt)
½ cup mashed potato
2¼ cups firmly packed brown sugar
3 large eggs
2½ cups all-purpose flour
2 tsp baking soda
½ tsp salt
½ cup buttermilk
1 cup boiling clear potato water
cherry pie filling (19 oz can)
whipped cream or whipped topping
chocolate curls (shaved semi-sweet chocolate)

Preheat oven to 350°F. Grease and flour three 8-inch cake pans or one 13x9-inch cake pan. (I prefer oblong pan as three layers makes a very high cake.) Cream melted chocolate, butter, potato and brown sugar until well-blended. Add eggs one at a time, beating after each addition. Sift together flour, baking soda and salt. Add dry ingredients to mixture alternately with buttermilk. Blend well. Fold in boiling potato water. Pour batter into prepared pans. Bake 25 minutes for layers and 40 to 45 minutes for oblong pan. When cool, cover with cherry pie filling. Spread with whipped cream and sprinkle with chocolate curls for garnish, if desired.

Chocolate-Pecan Cake

1 cup pecans, finely chopped
2 cups all-purpose flour
¾ tsp baking soda
¼ tsp salt
2 cups granulated sugar
¾ cup butter or margarine
2 tsp vanilla
4 eggs
¾ cup mashed potato
3 oz unsweetened chocolate, melted over hot water
⅔ cup buttermilk

Preheat oven to 350°F. Grease a 13x9-inch cake pan and line with waxed paper. Toss pecans in ¼ cup flour. Sift remaining flour, baking soda and salt. Cream butter and sugar. Add vanilla and eggs, adding one egg at a time and mixing well after each addition. Stir in potato and chocolate. Add sifted dry ingredients alternately with buttermilk, beginning and ending with dry ingredients. Fold in pecans. Bake 50 to 55 minutes. Cool.

Frosting
⅓ cup melted butter or margarine
¼ cup milk
3 tbsp cocoa
2½ to 3 cups icing sugar
1 tsp vanilla

Combine melted butter, milk and vanilla. Sift cocoa with 2 cups icing sugar. Add to mixture and beat well. Add extra icing sugar if necessary to make a spreading consistency.

The early Parliamentarians in England used potato flour as wig powder.

Festive Cake

A moist rich cake with that ever-popular chocolate flavour.

2 cups granulated sugar
¾ cup butter, margarine or shortening
4 eggs, separated
2 cups all-purpose flour
2 tsp baking powder
1 tsp cinnamon
1 tsp nutmeg
¼ tsp salt
¾ cup cocoa
1 cup mashed potato
½ cup milk
1 tsp vanilla
1 cup raisins
1 cup chopped walnuts

Preheat oven to 350°F. Grease and flour 10-inch tube pan. Cream sugar and butter. Add egg yolks and beat thoroughly. Sift together flour, baking powder, cinnamon, nutmeg, cocoa and salt. Coat raisins in small portion of flour mixture. Add potato to creamed mixture. Add flour mixture alternately with milk, beating after each addition, beginning and ending with flour. Add vanilla, raisins and nuts. Fold in stiffly beaten egg whites. Bake for 1 hour or until toothpick inserted in centre comes out dry. Cool, and frost if desired.

In some parts of the world, potatoes are a luxury. Philippine housewives sometimes top off their grocery bags with potatoes to show they are from an affluent family.

Potato Pound Cake

Beating for the specified amount of time is important for this cake's success. Pound cake is better if it has aged one or two days.

1 cup soft butter or margarine
1 cup granulated sugar
1 tsp grated lemon rind
1 tbsp lemon juice
4 large eggs
3/8 cup finely mashed potato
1/4 tsp nutmeg
1/4 tsp baking powder
15/8 cups all-purpose flour

Preheat oven to 325°F. Grease and lightly flour a 9x5x3-inch loaf pan. Cream butter thoroughly (1 minute). Add sugar gradually, creaming well after each addition (10 minutes). Mix in the lemon rind and juice (30 seconds). Beat in the eggs one at a time, beating for 1½ minutes with each egg. Add potato; mix well. Sift together and stir in the dry ingredients. Mix just until smooth (about 1 minute). Pour into prepared pan. Bake for 30 minutes, then reduce heat to 300°F and bake approximately 1 hour. Cool. Slice thinly and serve plain.

Cherry-Potato Pound Cake

Be sure to beat this batter the specified amount of time. A moist, attractive cake for afternoon tea and a nice alternative to fruit cakes at Christmas.

1 cup soft butter or margarine
1 cup fine granulated sugar
1 tsp grated lemon rind
1 tbsp freshly squeezed lemon juice
4 large eggs
½ cup riced potato
½ tsp almond extract
1/4 tsp double-acting baking powder
1½ cups presifted all-purpose flour
1 cup candied cherries (red and green) halved
2 tbsp all-purpose flour to lightly coat cherries

Grease a 9x5x3-inch loaf pan and line with waxed paper. Cream butter for one minute. Gradually add sugar, creaming well after each addition. Cream 10 minutes after last sugar is added. Mix in lemon rind and juice and beat 30 seconds. Beat in eggs one at a time, beating for 1 minute with each egg. Add potato and almond extract. Mix well. Sift dry ingredients. Gradually add to other mixture; mix just until smooth. Fold in floured cherries and pour into prepared pan. Let sit while pre-heating oven to 325°F. Bake for 30 minutes; reduce heat to 300°F and bake approximately 1 hour longer. Cool thoroughly before slicing. Slice thinly and serve plain.

Potato-Applesauce Cake

Combinations of potatoes and applesauce have long been favourites at home and abroad. Here they team up with oatmeal and spice to make a deliciously moist cake. Frost with Butter Cream Frosting and sprinkle with chopped nuts, if desired. My family likes this cake served hot with whipped cream for dessert.

½ cup butter or margarine
1 cup granulated sugar
1 egg
1½ cups all-purpose flour
1 tsp soda
½ tsp salt
1 tsp cinnamon
½ tsp cloves
⅔ cup grated potato (grated medium-coarse)
1 cup sweetened applesauce
½ cup chopped walnuts
1 cup rolled oats

Preheat oven to 350°F. Grease and flour an 8-inch quare cake pan. Beat butter until creamy; add sugar and egg, mixing well. Sift together all dry ingredients. Stir into the creamed mixture. Blend well. Combine potato, applesauce and chopped nuts. Stir into batter along with rolled oats. Pour into prepared pan and bake in preheated oven for 45 minutes. Let stand in pan 5 minutes before removing to a wire rack to cool. Frost if desired with Butter Cream Icing.

Potato-Cherry-Walnut Layer Cake

A light fluffy cake combining the flavours of maraschino cherries and walnuts.

4 egg whites
⅓ cup granulated sugar
2 cups all-purpose flour
3 tsp baking powder
¾ tsp salt
¾ cup shortening
1½ cups granulated sugar
1 cup mashed potato
4 egg yolks
1 tsp vanilla
1 cup milk
½ cup maraschino cherries, chopped finely
½ cup walnuts, grated or chopped in a blender

Preheat oven to 350°F. Grease and flour three 8-inch cake pans on the bottom only, (do not grease the sides of the pan). Beat egg whites until thick and foamy. Gradually add ⅓ cup sugar and beat until stiff. Set aside. Sift together flour, baking powder and salt. In a large mixing bowl cream shortening and gradually add remaining sugar; blend well. Add potato, egg yolks and vanilla. Beat until light and fluffy. Alternately add dry ingredients and milk, beginning and ending with dry ingredients. Fold in cherries and nuts along with the last addition of flour. Mix well. Gently fold in stiffly beaten egg whites. Put in prepared pans. Bake for 30 minutes. Ice with Butter Cream Icing.

Velvet Nut Cake

Mashed potatoes give this cake a beautiful, velvety texture.

1¾ cups all-purpose flour
1 tsp baking soda
½ tsp nutmeg
1 tsp cinnamon
½ tsp salt
1 cup mashed potato
1 cup buttermilk
¾ cup shortening
1½ cups brown sugar

3 eggs, separated
¾ cup chopped walnuts

Preheat oven to 350°F. Grease and flour two 8-inch cake pans. Combine flour, baking soda, nutmeg, cinnamon and salt. Set aside. Beat potato and buttermilk together until no lumps remain. Cream shortening, sugar and egg yolks until light. Add vanilla. Blend in dry ingredients gradually, alternating with potato/milk mixture, beginning and ending with dry ingredients. Fold in nuts and stiffly beaten egg whites. Pour batter into pans and bake 45 minutes, until a toothpick inserted in centre comes out dry.

Orange Potato Cake

A delicate light cake with a subtle orange flavour. Excellent for gluten-free diets. Be sure to follow the exact method of preparation and to use potato flour.

4 eggs
1 cup granulated sugar
½ cup potato flour
1 tsp baking powder
½ tsp salt
2 tbsp orange juice
grated rind of half an orange

Preheat oven to 325°F. Grease and line with waxed paper an 8-inch square cake pan. Beat eggs on high speed with a mixer until thick and smooth; gradually add sugar, beating until mixture resembles whipped cream. Sift together potato flour, baking powder and salt. Blend into egg mixture. Add orange juice and rind and mix thoroughly. Spread in cake pan. Bake for 15 minutes; increase heat to 350°F and bake an additional 15 minutes or until cake is firm. Cool on cake rack. Do not open oven door during the first 25 minutes of baking as this cake will fall easily.

Potatoes can be used in various ways and are considered one of the world's most versatile foods. Maybe this is why a "jack-of-all-trades" in India is called "alu," meaning potato.

Pioneer Potato Cake

You cannot substitute the potato flour and achieve the same results with this recipe. Potato flour can be obtained at most health food stores. A light and delicious cake, it is excellent served with strawberries and cream.

¾ cup potato flour
1 tsp baking powder
½ tsp salt
4 eggs
¾ cup granulated sugar
1 tsp vanilla
1 tsp lemon juice

Preheat oven to 350°F. Sift together flour, baking powder and salt. Mix eggs and sugar in a mixing bowl. Set bowl in a larger bowl containing hot water. Beat with an electric mixer until mixture is lukewarm. Remove from hot water and beat for 6 to 8 minutes. (Mixture is very light and fluffy, resembling whipped cream.) Add flavouring. Gradually fold in dry ingredients. Pour into an ungreased 8-inch tube pan. Bake for 40 minutes. Invert pan to cool.

Sponge Cake

Try this version of an old favourite, this time with potato flour. Again, be sure not to substitute the flour.

¾ cup sugar
½ cup potato flour
1 tsp baking powder
¼ tsp salt
4 egg whites
4 egg yolks
½ tsp lemon juice

Preheat oven to 350°F. Sift sugar, set aside. Sift flour with baking powder and salt. Beat egg whites until stiff, add 4 tbsp of the sugar; set aside. Beat egg yolks until thick and lemon-coloured. Beat in remaining sugar and lemon juice. Fold egg-white mixture into yolks. Mix in dry ingredients. Cut and fold into egg mixture. Do not beat. (Light mixing and folding will help avoid breaking air bubbles.) Bake in an ungreased 10-inch tube pan for 40 minutes.

Desserts

Every cook at some time or another wants to show off—to do something daring and dramatic. Here is your chance to serve potatoes for dessert. In this chapter you will find recipes for pies (North America's favourite dessert) as well as shortcakes, puddings and gingerbread.

Whether plain or fancy, desserts are the crowning glory of any table.

Potato Maple-Walnut Pie

pastry for single-crust 9-inch pie
½ cup butter or margarine
1 cup brown sugar
1 cup Potato Maple Syrup (see Miscellaneous)
4 eggs, slightly beaten
pinch salt
1 tsp vanilla
1 cup chopped walnuts

Preheat oven to 375°F. Line pie plate with pastry. Combine all ingredients. Mix well. Bake 40 minutes, until centre is firm.
Serves 6.

Variation: Try Potato Pecan Pie, substituting pecans for walnuts.

Potato Syrup Pie

pastry for single-crust 9-inch pie
¾ cup raisins
2 tbsp butter or margarine
1 egg
¾ cup Potato Maple Syrup (see Miscellaneous)
¾ cup brown sugar
½ cup peanut butter
¼ tsp salt
1 tsp vanilla
½ cup evaporated milk

Preheat oven to 400°F. Line pie plate with pastry. Sprinkle with raisins. Beat butter, egg, syrup, sugar, peanut butter, salt, vanilla and milk with electric mixer. Pour over raisins. Bake 15 minutes; reduce heat to 325°F and bake 45 minutes. Cool completely. Serve with whipped cream. *Serves 6.*

Note: This filling can be used for tarts (makes 12 tarts).

Mid-Winter Pie

A combination of apples, potatoes and cranberries that is sure to be a favourite. Serve with ice cream or whipped cream.

pastry for double-crust 9-inch pie.
1 cup grated raw potato (medium-fine)
1½ cups peeled apple, coarsely grated
1½ cups raw cranberries
½ cup water
⅔ cup granulated sugar
2 tbsp all-purpose flour
½ cup corn syrup or Potato Maple Syrup (see Miscellaneous)
⅛ tsp salt
1 tsp grated orange rind

In medium saucepan cook potato, apple and cranberries in water until cranberries pop. Watch closely as this mixture will burn easily. Stir in sugar. Remove from heat, cover and cool to room temperature. Preheat oven to 425°F. Combine flour, syrup, salt and orange rind. Stir into potato mixture. Pour into pastry-lined pie plate. Cover with lattice top. Bake 40 minutes.
Serves 6.

Lemony Potato Pie

An unusually tasty Early American dessert. This pie is very rich. Serve with whipped cream.

pastry for single-crust 9-inch pie
4 medium potatoes, peeled and sliced thinly
1½ cups granulated sugar
juice of 1 lemon
¼ cup potato water
½ cup dark brown sugar
1 tbsp butter or margarine

Boil potato slices in water until barely tender. Remove from water with a slotted spoon, taking care not to break them; save potato water. Stir sugar, lemon juice and ¼ cup reserved potato water in saucepan. Simmer for 5 minutes, stirring occasionally. Carefully add the potato slices to the lemon-sugar syrup. Bring to a boil. Remove from heat and cool. Preheat oven to 425°F. Line a 9-inch pie plate with pastry. Arrange cooled potato slices over the crust and pour syrup over. Sprinkle with brown sugar, dot with butter and bake 15 minutes; reduce heat to 350°F and bake 30 to 35 minutes longer. Serve at room temperature or chilled. *Serves 6.*

Lemon-Custard Potato Pie

pastry for single-crust 9-inch pie (partially cooked for 6 to 8 minutes)
½ cup warm mashed potato
2 tbsp butter or margarine
2 egg whites
¾ cup granulated sugar
2 egg yolks
juice of ½ lemon
1 tbsp finely grated lemon rind
½ cup milk

Preheat oven to 400°F. Whip potato and butter with electric mixer until smooth. Cool. Beat egg whites until stiff peaks form. To potato/butter mixture add sugar, egg yolks, lemon juice, lemon rind and milk. Blend thoroughly. Fold in egg whites. Put in partially cooked pastry shell. Bake 25 to 30 minutes.
Serves 6.

Irish Apple Pie

A delicious apple dessert from Ireland. The pastry is not as firm as
regular pastry. Be sure to grease the pie pan.

2 cups hot mashed potato
1 tbsp butter or margarine
⅛ tsp cinnamon
⅛ tsp ginger
1 tbsp brown sugar
¼ cup all-purpose flour
4 cups thinly sliced apples
2 tbsp brown sugar
1 tsp melted butter or margarine
1 tsp granulated sugar

Preheat oven to 375°F. Combine potato, butter, cinnamon, ginger and
brown sugar. Mix well. Blend in flour. Reserve ¾ cup for top of the pie.
On a sheet of waxed paper, pat the remaining dough into a circle slightly
larger than a 9-inch pie plate. Place a well-greased pie plate over dough.
Lift and invert the dough into the pan. Remove waxed paper. Arrange
apple slices over potato mixture. Sprinkle with 2 tbsp brown sugar. Pat
remaining ¾ cup of potato mixture onto a 9-inch circle of waxed paper.
Invert over pie. Peel off paper, crimp and seal edges of dough around
pie. Cut a vent in the centre of the pie. Bake 45 to 50 minutes. Brush
top with 1 tsp melted butter and sprinkle with granulated sugar a few
minutes before removing from oven. Serve hot with whipped cream.
Serves 6.

Mincemeat-and-Potato Pie

A delicious mincemeat pie with creamy potato topping.

pastry for single-crust 9-inch pie
1 cup mashed potato
1 cup evaporated milk
½ cup brown sugar
1 egg, slightly beaten
½ tsp salt
¼ tsp cinnamon
¼ tsp ginger
1 tsp grated lemon rind
1 tbsp butter or margarine
2 cups prepared mincemeat*

Preheat oven to 450°F. Combine potato, milk, brown sugar, egg, salt, cinnamon, ginger and lemon rind. Cook over low heat for 3 to 4 minutes, stirring constantly (until slightly thickened). Stir in butter. Put mincemeat in bottom of pastry-lined pie plate; top with potato mixture. Bake for 15 minutes. Reduce heat to 350°F and bake 30 minutes longer. *Serves 6.*

* Green tomato mincemeat works, too.

Potato Maple-Butter Tarts

pastry for 12 tart shells
boiling water or potato water
½ cup raisins
½ cup butter or margarine
½ cup brown sugar
¼ tsp salt
½ cup Potato Maple Syrup (see Miscellaneous)
1 beaten egg
½ tsp vanilla
few drops lemon juice

Preheat oven to 350°F. Pour boiling water over raisins and let soak until edges turn white. Drain. Meanwhile, cream butter, add sugar and mix well. Beat in remaining ingredients. Add raisins. Fill tart shells ⅔ full. Bake 20 minutes. Do not let filling boil. *Makes 12 tarts.*

Potato-Rhubarb Delight

Tangy rhubarb with a rich and delicious biscuit topping.

3 cups chopped rhubarb
½ cup granulated sugar
1 cup all-purpose flour
1½ tsp baking powder
¼ tsp salt
¼ cup granulated sugar
⅜ cup butter or margarine
1 cup sieved or riced cooked potato

Preheat oven to 400°F. Wash rhubarb well and place in a 9-inch pie plate. Add sugar and bake for 15 minutes. (Dot with butter and add a pinch of salt if desired.) Meanwhile, combine flour, baking powder, salt and sugar. Cut in butter. Stir in potato. Knead to form a dough. Roll out to ½-inch thickness on a lightly floured board. Cut in circles with a biscuit cutter. Remove fruit from oven. Drain off juice and save. Pour back ¼ cup of juice; discard remaining juice or save to use later in muffins or a jellied salad. Cover fruit with circles of biscuit. Bake 15 minutes or until golden brown. Serve hot with sweetened whipped cream.
Serves 6.

Potato Gingerbread

This gingerbread keeps well. It may be served with whipped cream or Foamy Egg Sauce (see Centennial Pudding). Raisins may also be added to the mixture.

⅝ cup shortening
½ cup granulated sugar
2 eggs
1 cup molasses
½ cup finely mashed potato
2⅛ cups all-purpose flour
2 tsp baking powder
1 tsp cinnamon
1 tsp ginger
½ tsp salt
1 cup hot potato water or water

Preheat oven to 350°F. Lightly grease and flour a 9x9-inch cake pan. Cream shortening; add sugar and cream together until well-blended. Add eggs and molasses and beat thoroughly. Blend in potato. Sift together flour, baking powder, cinnamon, ginger and salt. Add to the potato mixture and beat only until smooth. Add the hot water and mix until well-blended. Bake 40 minutes.
Serves 9.

Grandma's Apple Cake

A delicious dessert served with whipped cream or cooled and iced with a butter icing.

¾ cup butter or margarine
⅔ cup sugar
2 eggs, beaten
⅔ cup hot mashed potato
1¾ cups all-purpose flour
½ tsp salt
1 tbsp baking powder
½ tsp cinnamon
2 medium cooking apples (peel and slice thinly when ready to use*)

Preheat oven to 350°F. Grease and flour an 8-inch square cake pan. Cream butter, sugar and eggs until light. Blend in potato. Combine flour, salt, baking powder and cinnamon. Fold into butter mixture, blending until well-mixed. Fold in sliced apples. Pour batter into prepared pan and bake 45 to 50 minutes.

* Do not peel apples ahead as they will darken.

A "Potato Monument" stands at the site of a ruined castle in Hirchhorn, in the Neckar Valley. The inscription reads: "To God and Francis Drake, who brought to Europe for the everlasting benefit of the poor—the potato."

All-Seasons Shortcake

Strawberries, raspberries, blueberries and other fruits such as apples, peaches and rhubarb may be used with this recipe. This recipe comes from the P.E.I. Potato Marketing Board.

1 cup all-purpose flour
2 tsp baking powder
¼ tsp salt
¼ cup granulated sugar
⅜ cup butter or margarine
1 cup mashed potato
¾ cup berries
¼ cup sugar
½ cup whipping cream

Preheat oven to 400°F. Combine flour, baking powder, salt and sugar in a mixing bowl. Cut in butter until mixture is crumbly. Stir in potato. Knead to form a dough and roll out to 1-inch thickness on a lightly floured board. Cut into circles with a biscuit cutter. Bake 15 minutes or until golden brown. Mash ⅔ cup berries (save a few for garnish). Strain the liquid (especially important with raspberries). Add 3 tbsp sugar to berries. When biscuits are cool, split in two. Place 1½ tbsp berries on bottom of each biscuit. Whip cream with about 2 tsp sugar. Spread cream on biscuit and cover with the biscuit top. Garnish with a small amount of whipped cream and a few whole berries.
Serves 6.

An annual festival in O'Leary, Prince Edward Island, is held in July to coincide with the times when potato fields are in bloom. It is called the "Potato Blossom Festival."

Centennial Pudding (with Foamy Egg Sauce)

A recipe from the P.E.I. Potato Marketing Board. Definitely a celebration-day pudding. May be cooked ahead and reheated for serving.

½ cup ground suet
½ cup brown sugar
½ cup molasses
1½ cups grated carrot
1 cup grated raw potato
1 cup all-purpose flour
1 tsp baking soda
½ tsp salt
1 tsp cinnamon
⅛ tsp ground cloves
½ tsp nutmeg
½ tsp allspice
1 cup chopped raisins
⅓ cup chopped candied orange peel or citron

Combine suet, sugar, molasses, grated carrot and potato. Mix well. Sift together flour, baking soda, salt, cinnamon, cloves, nutmeg and allspice. Add to first mixture and stir well. Add raisins and chopped fruit. Fill a well-greased 1½-quart pudding mold two-thirds full. Cover lightly and steam for 3 to 3½ hours. Serve with Foamy Egg Sauce.
Serves 10 to 12.

Foamy Egg Sauce
4 egg yolks
1 cup icing sugar
¾ tsp vanilla or rum flavouring
pinch salt
1½ cups whipping cream

Beat egg yolks, icing sugar, flavouring and salt. Whip cream; fold into mixture. Chill. Stir before serving.
Makes 4 cups.

Steamed Potato Pudding (with Lemon Sauce)

From the kitchen of Pauline Essery, Summerside, P.E.I.

½ cup shortening
1 cup granulated sugar
1 cup grated raw potato
1¼ cups grated raw carrot
1 cup all-purpose flour
1 tsp baking soda
1 tsp salt
1 tsp cinnamon
½ tsp cloves
1 cup raisins
⅓ cup candied citron peel

Cream shortening and sugar. Add vegetables. Mix dry ingredients and fruit. Add to the above mixture and blend well. Press lightly into a greased pudding mold. Cover loosely with tin foil lightly and steam for 2¼ hours. Serve warm with Lemon Sauce. (The pudding also freezes well; it will keep up to six months in a freezer. Thaw and reheat in 325°F oven for 20 minutes, or steam for the same length of time.)

Lemon Sauce
¼ cup granulated sugar
1 tbsp cornstarch
few grains salt
1 cup cold water (can use leftover potato water)
2 tbsp lemon juice
2 tbsp butter or margarine

Mix dry ingredients; add cold water. Cook over low heat until thickened, stirring constantly. Add lemon juice and butter. Pour over pudding. *Serves 10 to 12.*

The headmaster of a cooking school in Dardilly, France, requires each of his students to prepare sixty potato dishes before graduation.

Potato Christmas Pudding
(with Brown Sugar Rum Sauce)

Adapted from the CIP International Potato Cookbook published in Peru by the International Potato Centre Women's Club (Las Damas del CIP). This dessert can be made in advance and reheated in the oven or in a steamer.

½ cup shortening
1 cup granulated sugar
1 cup grated raw potato
1½ cups grated raw carrot
1 cup all-purpose flour
1 tsp baking soda
1 tsp salt
1 tsp cinnamon
½ tsp cloves
½ cup seedless raisins
½ cup diced candied fruit

Cream together shortening and sugar. Add potato and carrot. Sift dry ingredients and combine with raisins and fruit. Mix all ingredients together. Fill greased 1½-quart pudding mold three-quarters full; cover lightly with aluminum foil. Steam 2½ hours. Unmold. Serve hot with Brown Sugar Rum Sauce.
Serves 10 to 12.

Brown Sugar Rum Sauce
¾ cup brown sugar
dash salt
1½ tbsp all-purpose flour
1½ cups boiling water or potato water
2 tbsp margarine or butter
⅓ cup rum

Mix sugar, salt and flour in a saucepan. Add boiling water slowly. Cook and stir over direct heat until smooth and slightly thickened. Simmer 5 minutes. Remove from heat and add butter and rum. Stir until well-mixed. Pour hot over pudding.

Baked Lemon-and-Potato Pudding

A cake-type pudding with a rich lemon sauce. The sauce makes itself!

1½ cups granulated sugar
⅓ cup all-purpose flour
¼ cup potato flour
½ tsp salt
1½ tbsp grated lemon rind
⅓ cup lemon juice
3 egg yolks, beaten
3 tsp soft butter or margarine
1½ cups milk
3 egg whites

Preheat oven to 350°F. Combine sugar, flour, potato flour and salt. Stir in lemon rind, lemon juice, egg yolks, butter and milk. Fold in stiffly beaten egg whites. Pour into a buttered 2-quart casserole. Set in a pan of hot water in oven. Bake 45 to 50 minutes.
Serves 6.

Ohio Potato Pudding

A nineteenth-century potato and carrot pudding served with Brown Sugar Rum Sauce (see Potato Christmas Pudding).

1 cup grated raw potato
1 cup grated raw carrot
1 cup currants
1 cup raisins
1 cup sugar (granulated or brown)
1 cup all-purpose flour
2 tsp baking soda
1 tsp salt

Combine vegetables and fruit. Thoroughly mix all other ingredients. Combine two mixtures and blend thoroughly. Place in a large pudding mold. Cover pudding bowl with foil wrap. Place on a rack in a large cooking pot; add boiling water, 1 to 2 inches deep. Cover pot; steam 3 hours, adding water if needed. Cool 10 minutes; unmold. Serve warm with Brown Sugar Rum Sauce or any desired pudding sauce.
Serves 8.

Orange Potato Pudding (with Vanilla Sauce)

4 egg yolks
⅓ cup granulated sugar
⅓ cup ground blanched almonds
2 tbsp orange juice
1 tbsp grated orange rind
1 cup mashed potato
4 egg whites

Preheat oven to 350°F. Beat egg yolks and sugar until thick and lemon-coloured. Add almonds, orange juice and rind. Beat in mashed potato. Whip egg whites until stiff and fold into potato mixture. Pour into a mold that has been lined with waxed paper. Place in a pan of hot water. Bake 45 minutes. Remove and cool 5 minutes. Unmold on serving platter. Serve with Vanilla Sauce.
Serves 6.

Vanilla Sauce
½ pkg (3¾ oz) vanilla pudding
1 cup milk
1 egg yolk
2 tbsp orange juice
1 tbsp grated orange rind
1 tsp rum flavouring (optional)

Combine pudding with milk and egg yolk. Cook over medium heat, stirring constantly until it thickens and begins to bubble. Add remaining ingredients. Stir. Pour over warm pudding.

Apple-and-Potato Cottage Pudding

The German people were the first to combine apples with potatoes.
They called potatoes "earth apples," much as the French called them
"Pommes de terre". . .apples of the earth.

6 medium tart apples, peeled and sliced
3 tbsp brown sugar
3 tbsp melted butter or margarine
1½ cups all-purpose flour
½ cup mashed potato
1½ tsp baking powder
½ tsp salt
¼ cup shortening
¾ cup granulated sugar
1 egg
¾ cup milk
1 tbsp granulated sugar
1 tsp cinnamon

Preheat oven to 350°F. Grease a 9-inch square cake pan. Combine apples,
brown sugar and melted butter. Spread in prepared cake pan. Combine
flour, potato, baking powder and salt. Cream shortening and sugar;
add egg and beat well. Gradually add flour mixture alternately with
milk. Pour over apples. Sprinkle with a mixture of cinnamon and sugar.
Bake 45 minutes. Serve with whipped cream.
Serves 6.

Candy

Contrary to popular belief, many candies can be made at home without using special equipment. Over the years candy-making has become associated with special occasions. At our house we have good, old-fashioned candy-making sessions at Christmas and Easter. The best and most special occasions, though, are the unexpected ones. When the wind howls and snow swirls around until you cannot see the house next door, it's time to make candy. This practice has gone on for over a quarter-century. Snowtime is candy time—candy sweetens the gloomiest day. And by using potatoes we add nutrition to a favourite treat.

Irish Potato Candy

½ cup cold mashed potato
¼ tsp salt
½ tsp vanilla
4 cups icing sugar (approximately)
1 cup peanut butter

Combine mashed potato, salt and vanilla. Add enough icing sugar to make the mixture leave the sides of the bowl. Knead on a pastry board, using extra icing sugar as necessary. Divide dough and roll in two rectangles. Spread ½ cup peanut butter on each rectangle. Roll in jelly roll fashion. Wrap in waxed paper and refrigerate at least 2 hours. To serve, slice in thin slices.

Polish Potato Bonbons

¾ cup warm mashed potato
4 cups icing sugar
4 cups flaked coconut
1½ cups semi-sweet chocolate chips
1 square bittersweet chocolate
2 oz (½ cake) paraffin wax

Blend together the mashed potato, sugar and coconut. Form into balls the size of a small walnut. Melt chocolate and paraffin in a double boiler. Dip the potato balls into the chocolate mixture. Drain on waxed paper and let cool until firm.

Variation: In place of chocolate bits of cherry, lemon or caramel pieces can be used.

Chocolate Crunch Candy

1 cup crunchy peanut butter
2 tbsp butter or margarine
½ cup mashed potato
½ tsp salt
1 cup coconut
1 cup Rice Krispies
2 cups icing sugar

Cream peanut butter, butter and mashed potato. Add salt, coconut, Rice Krispies and icing sugar. Mix well. Form into small balls.

Chocolate Dip
8 oz chocolate chips
½ bar paraffin wax

Melt chocolate chips and paraffin over hot water. Dip candy in chocolate mixture and cool on waxed paper. Store in refrigerator.

Icing sugar measurements for candy recipes are approximate as the amount required will vary according to the type (and wetness) of potato used.

Potato Chocolates

These chocolates can be made in a variety of flavours.

1 cup riced potato
1 tbsp butter or margarine
1 tsp flavouring of your choice
5 to 5½ cups icing sugar

Combine riced potato and butter. Beat with electric mixer or wooden spoon until light. Add flavouring and gradually work in icing sugar. Mixture should be a smooth firm dough. (I often mix in sugar before flavouring and then divide mixture into several small bowls. I then use a variety of flavourings and put a few drops in each dish. I sometimes use different food colourings to match the flavours.) Knead dough on a board. Form into small balls or shapes. Bits of nuts or cherries may be added.

Chocolate Dip
4 oz semi-sweet chocolate*
1-inch square paraffin wax
2 tbsp butter or margarine
5 drops vanilla

Melt chocolate, wax and butter in top of a double boiler. Stir until blended. Add vanilla. Heat mixture to 130°F then cool to 83°F. Keeping the temperatures between 83°F and 85°F, dip chocolates into mixture and coat thoroughly. Lift out carefully with two forks. Place on a rack covered with waxed paper. Draw a skewer across dipped candy to form a thread—the mark of an expert chocolate dipper. (If chocolate hardens, it can be melted, cooled to 83°F and reused.)

* Use your choice of chocolate. I prefer semi-sweet or a mixture of 2 oz semi-sweet and 2 oz unsweetened.

Napoleon's army had exceptionally good dental health. Their diet consisted mainly of potatoes.

After-Dinner Mints

1 medium potato, peeled and quartered
2 tbsp milk
1 tsp salt
1 tsp vanilla
8 cups sifted icing sugar
food colouring
spearmint flavouring to taste (available in health food stores)

Boil potato in a small amount of water. When tender, remove cover and boil out all water. Beat until fluffy with an electric mixer. Add milk, salt and vanilla. Slowly add sugar until mixture is very thick. Divide into 3 or 4 portions. Add desired food colouring and flavouring to each portion. Drop by teaspoons onto waxed paper or push through a cookie press. Let stand until firm. Store in an airtight container or freeze.

Chocolate-Covered Peppermint Patties

At our house it wouldn't be Christmas without Peppermint Patties!

1 cup mashed potato
5 cups icing sugar
1 tsp salt
2 tbsp melted butter or margarine
2 tsp peppermint extract

Cream potato, sugar, salt, butter and peppermint extract. Knead slightly. Form into balls the size of cherries. Flatten balls to form circles. Let dry overnight at room temperature.

Chocolate Coating
8 squares semi-sweet chocolate
½ bar paraffin wax

Melt semi-sweet chocolate and paraffin in top of a double boiler. Keep melted over hot water. (Do not heat too hot.) Dip patties in chocolate and let cool on waxed paper.

Potato Coconut Fudge

1 cup hot mashed potato
pinch of salt
2 tsp soft butter or margarine
1 lb icing sugar
1 tsp vanilla
1 lb coconut
2 oz melted semi-sweet chocolate

Sprinkle salt over potato and spread with butter. Spoon into icing sugar and stir until very well blended. Add vanilla and coconut. Put in a 9x12-inch cake pan. Dribble with melted chocolate.

Variation: Use bitter chocolate or melted chocolate-mint chips for a different taste.

Quick Chocolate-Potato Fudge

3 squares chocolate (2 sweet and 1 unsweetened)
3 tbsp butter or margarine
⅓ cup mashed potato
⅛ tsp salt
1 tsp vanilla
4 cups sifted icing sugar (approximate)

Melt chocolate and butter over hot water. Add the mashed potato, salt and vanilla. Blend in sugar. Knead until smooth. Shape into a long roll about 1 inch in diameter. Cool and cut into slices.

Variations: Try 3 ounces of semi-sweet chocolate chips instead of the squares. You can also use butterscotch, peanut butter or chocolate mint.

"Curiosity and interest are immediately aroused when you put into a young person's hands, a potato." —*Louis Pasteur*

Easter Eggs

For many years, these were the only Easter eggs to arrive at our house.

½ cup mashed potato
8 cups icing sugar
½ cup soft butter or margarine
vanilla or peppermint flavouring (or your choice)
1 egg white
chopped cherries, if desired
chopped walnuts, if desired
food colourings
1 pkg (8-oz) semi-sweet chocolate
1-inch square paraffin wax

Whip potato until very creamy. Add icing sugar, butter and desired flavouring to taste. Blend in egg white and mix thoroughly. Set aside about one-third of mixture for "egg yolks." Add cherries or nuts to remaining mixture if desired. Blend thoroughly. To shape eggs, place a small amount of yellow mixture in centre of each egg for a "yolk." Cover with other mixture. Form in egg shape approximately 1½ inches in diameter. Refrigerate until thoroughly cooled. Melt chocolate and paraffin over hot water in a double boiler. Dip chilled eggs in chocolate mixture to cover completely. Set on waxed paper to cool. When completely cooled these eggs can be decorated with children's names, flowers, etc. made from decorator's icing.

Strawberry Spuds

½ cup mashed potato
1½ cups icing sugar
¼ tsp salt
1 tbsp soft butter or margarine
strawberry jello

Combine potato, icing sugar, salt and butter. Mix well. Form in strawberry shapes. Roll in jello powder. Garnish with green decorator's icing. Place a coloured toothpick in the end of the "strawberry" for a stem.

Variations: Form candy in various shapes and dust with different flavours of jello.

Patsy's Potato Bars

Deliciously rich, the mixture is very stiff and must be pressed into the pan.

1 cup mashed potato at room temperature
8 cups sifted icing sugar
½ tsp salt
½ cup soft butter or margarine
3 cups unsweetened coconut
2 tsp vanilla
1 cup semi-sweet chocolate chips

Mix potato, icing sugar, salt, butter, coconut and vanilla. Press firmly into a 9x13-inch cake pan. Drizzle with melted chocolate chips. Refrigerate. Cut in bars.

Variation: Divide mixture into two 8-inch pans. Drizzle with melted butterscotch chips, peanut butter chips or mint chocolate.

Chunky Peanut-Potato Pinwheels

Do not make this recipe on a humid or wet day as candy will not firm properly.

⅓ cup cold mashed potato
¼ cup butter or margarine
1 tsp vanilla
5 cups icing sugar
1 cup chunky peanut butter

Combine potato, butter and vanilla. Blend well. Gradually add icing sugar. Knead. Roll between two sheets of waxed paper to about ½-inch thickness and the width of the waxed paper. Remove top sheet of waxed paper and spread peanut butter over the mixture. Roll up like a jelly roll. Leave wrapped in the waxed paper. Chill 2 to 3 hours. To serve, cut in small slices and serve at once.

Many of those beautiful cones of ice cream we see advertised on television are, in fact, fluffy mashed potatoes.

Potato Fondant Dainties

Colourful and delicious!

1 cup mashed potato
1 tbsp butter or margarine
flavouring and food colouring of your choice
5 to 5½ cups icing sugar

Combine all ingredients and knead well. Form into desired shapes and decorate. Refrigerate.

Shapes and flavouring ideas:

Banana	yellow food colouring	mini-banana shape
Strawberry	red food colouring	strawberry shape
Maple	top with walnut pieces	
Almond	top with cherry bits	
Mint	green food colouring	

Potato-Peppermint Pinwheels

A favourite at our house at Christmas.

½ cup mashed potato
1 tsp vegetable oil
1 tsp peppermint extract
pinch of salt
5 cups sifted icing sugar
few drops of red or green food colouring

Combine mashed potato, vegetable oil, peppermint extract and salt. Beat well. Gradually add icing sugar to form a stiff dough. Divide into two dishes. Put a few drops of red or green food colouring in one dish. Knead both portions well. Roll as thinly as possible on plastic wrap. Place the white portion over the coloured one and press together firmly. Roll tightly as for jelly roll. Wrap in plastic wrap and chill at least 2 hours. Cut in ¼-inch slices. Set on cookie sheet or waxed paper to dry for several hours. Store at room temperature in an airtight container.

A Scandinavian man lived healthily for three hundred days on potatoes and a small amount of margarine.

Salads

Salads are no longer an eighteenth-century sun-season picnic dish. Equally popular for last-minute meals or make-ahead dinners, salads are becoming a year-round favourite. Salads may be an appetizer or an accompaniment or a meal in itself.

Salads are usually made from cooked or raw vegetables served with dressings and combinations of meats, fish, poultry and eggs. They can be plain or garnished.

No picnic, barbecue or Sunday family gathering would be complete without potato salad. Every country has its own special recipe. Here you will find a selection of the potato salads I have tried. All were equally delicious.

Note: Once salad dressing has been added to potato salad, keep the salad well-chilled or serve immediately. You risk food poisoning by holding potato salads at room temperature.

Green Bean and Potato Salad

A deliciously different potato salad.

3 lbs new potatoes
3 oz white wine or 1 oz white wine vinegar
¼ cup chicken broth
½ cup French Oil and Vinegar Dressing
¾ tsp summer savory
¾ tsp basil
1½ lbs fresh green beans, cut in 1-inch pieces
salt and pepper to taste

Scrub potatoes. Steam in small amount of water until just tender. Cool slightly and cut in quarters. While still warm, combine with wine and chicken broth and let stand for 20 minutes. Drain off any remaining liquid. Add French dressing, savory and basil, and toss lightly. Chill covered for at least 4 hours. Steam beans until just tender. Chill under running water, pat dry on paper towels and refrigerate 4 hours. Add beans to potatoes; season with salt and pepper and toss gently.
Serves 10 to 12.

French Oil and Vinegar Dressing
¾ cup vegetable oil
¼ cup vinegar
1 tbsp sugar
½ tsp salt
pinch pepper

Combine in a glass jar, cover and shake.

Curried Potato Salad

6 large potatoes
½ cup Italian dressing
1 cup chopped onion
2 cups mayonnaise
1 tbsp curry powder
½ tsp salt
1 tbsp chopped parsley

Boil, peel and dice potatoes. Cool. Add remaining ingredients and toss lightly. Chill.
Serves 6 to 8.

Italian Dressing
1 cup vegetable oil
⅓ cup vinegar
2 tbsp lemon juice
2 tsp sugar
½ tsp garlic salt
½ tsp dry mustard
½ tsp oregano
pinch of pepper

Combine in a glass jar. Cover and shake well. Store in refrigerator. Shake before using.
Makes 1½ cups.

Savory Potato Salad

6 medium potatoes, cooked, peeled and cubed
½ tsp savory
¼ tsp marjoram
¼ cup vegetable oil
¼ cup vinegar
salt to taste
¼ tsp pepper
½ cup minced onion
1 cup seeded and diced cucumber
½ cup mayonnaise
2 tbsp prepared mustard
cucumber, tomato, radish and lettuce for garnish, if desired

Place potatoes in a large bowl. Combine savory, marjoram, oil, vinegar, salt and pepper in a jar; shake well to blend. Pour over potatoes and let stand 1 hour. Add onion, cucumber, mayonnaise and mustard. Stir gently until thoroughly mixed. Garnish as desired.
Serves 6.

Cottage Cheese Potato Salad

1 cup cottage cheese
4 cups diced cooked potato
3 tbsp chopped sweet pickle
⅓ cup chopped green onion
½ cup chopped celery
¼ cup chopped green pepper
2 hard-cooked eggs, chopped
1 tsp salt
¼ tsp pepper
1 tsp dry mustard
⅓ to ½ cup mayonnaise or salad dressing

Combine cheese, potatoes, pickle, green onion, celery, green pepper and eggs. Mix together mustard, seasonings and mayonnaise. Pour over salad and toss lightly. Chill thoroughly before serving.
Makes 6 to 8 servings.

Slender P.E.I. Potato Salad

This light and refreshing salad has a touch of curry. A winning addition to your buffet table or a pleasant alternative to the more traditional potato salad. And it's low-calorie besides!

1 cup plain yogurt
2 tsp prepared mustard
1 tsp curry powder
2 cups cubed cooked potatoes
1 cup sliced and quartered cucumber
½ cup sliced celery
¼ cup chopped onion
1 tbsp chopped chives
salt and pepper to taste

In a large bowl, combine yogurt, mustard and curry. Add remaining ingredients; toss to mix well. Refrigerate for a few hours to blend flavours. Garnish with parsley flakes and fresh tomato wedges.
Makes 8 servings (½ cup), about 55 calories each.

Shrimp-and-Potato Salad

1 cup chopped cooked shrimp
3 tbsp vinegar or juice from sweet pickled gherkins
2 cups diced cooked potato
1 cup cooked peas, fresh or frozen
½ cup diced apple
3 gherkins or sweet pickles, chopped
1 tsp salt
¼ tsp pepper
1 tbsp prepared mustard
2 tbsp finely fresh chopped parsley
½ cup mayonnaise

Pour vinegar over shrimp. Let stand 10 minutes. Drain, saving vinegar. Mix shrimp with remaining ingredients. Stir in vinegar. Mix well. Chill 1 hour in refrigerator.
Serves 4.

Seafarer's Salad

Being a fisherman's daughter, I couldn't make a collection of salads without this old favourite that features potato chips and sardines.

2 medium heads lettuce
¼ cup grated cheddar cheese
¼ cup parmesan cheese
1 egg (raw)
¾ cup French dressing
2 (4 oz) cans sardines, drained
3 cups slightly broken potato chips

Break lettuce in small chunks. Sprinkle with cheese. Combine egg and French Dressing. Add to lettuce and cheese. Toss thoroughly. Add sardines and potato chips. Toss again lightly. Serve at once.
Serves 8.

French Dressing
¾ cup vegetable oil
¼ cup lemon juice
½ cup honey
½ tsp celery salt
½ tsp salt
¼ tsp paprika
¼ tsp dry mustard
¼ tsp pepper

Combine all ingredients in a glass jar. Cover and shake well. Store in refrigerator. Shake before using.
Makes 1 cup.

Party Potato Salad

Great for summer barbecues.

10 cups sliced cooked potato
¼ cup vegetable oil
½ cup wine vinegar
1 tsp salt
⅛ tsp pepper
1 tsp chives
8 slices bacon, cooked until crisp, then crumbled
4 hard-cooked eggs, diced
1 cup sliced celery
¼ cup chopped onion
¼ cup chopped green pepper
½ cup sour cream
½ cup mayonnaise
2 unpeeled cucumbers, scored with a fork lengthwise and sliced thinly

Combine potatoes, vegetable oil, vinegar, salt, pepper and chives. Mix
and chill. Add remaining ingredients at serving time. Mix lightly.
Serves 10 to 12.

Sausage-and-Potato Salad

6 to 8 medium potatoes, peeled, cooked and cubed
8 sausages, cooked and cut in quarters
½ cup mayonnaise
⅓ cup sour cream
1 tbsp vinegar
1 green onion, finely chopped
½ tsp dry mustard
½ tsp tarragon
½ tsp salt
pepper to taste

Place potatoes and sausages in a large bowl. Stir together remaining
ingredients; pour over potatoes and sausages. Toss lightly. Serve with
greens.
Serves 6 to 8.

Meat-and-Potato Salad Mold

A special make-ahead summer salad.

Meat Layer
2 cups finely ground cooked meat (ham, chicken or luncheon meat)
3 tbsp minced onion
⅔ cup mayonnaise
½ cup chili sauce
2 tsp prepared mustard
¼ tsp Tabasco sauce
¼ tsp celery salt
1 envelope unflavoured gelatin
½ cup cold water

Combine meat, onion, mayonnaise, chili sauce, mustard, Tabasco sauce and celery salt. Soften gelatin in cold water; heat over hot water until dissolved. Blend into meat mixture. Turn into an 8-cup salad mold. Chill until almost firm, approximately 1 hour.

Potato Layer
3 cups diced cooked potato
1 cup finely chopped celery
¼ cup chopped onion
¼ cup chopped green pepper
⅔ cup mayonnaise
1 tbsp vinegar
1 tsp salt
⅛ tsp pepper
1 envelope unflavoured gelatin
½ cup cold water

Combine potato, celery, onion, green pepper, mayonnaise, vinegar, salt and pepper. Soften gelatin in cold water. Dissolve over hot water. Blend into potato mixture. Spread over meat mixture. Chill until firm. *Serves 8.*

Raw potatoes are said to cure warts. I recently asked an elderly lady if this remedy worked. She assured me it did . . . if you used a stolen potato and were sure to bury it after application.

Molded Potato Salad

1 pkg lemon jello
¾ cup boiling water
½ cup cider vinegar
½ medium green pepper, chopped
1 cup mayonnaise
2 cups cubed cooked potato
1 stick celery, diced
1 tbsp choppped red pepper
2 hard-cooked eggs, chopped
salt and pepper to taste

Dissolve jello in boiling water and add vinegar. Chill until thick but not set. Beat in mayonnaise. Fold in remaining ingredients. Add salt and pepper. Pour into 1½-quart mold. Chill until set, approximately 1 hour. Unmold on bed of lettuce.
Serves 6.

Italian Potato Salad

1 cup diced cooked potato
1 cup diced and peeled apple
½ cup diced pickled cucumber (sweet or dill)
¾ cup chopped cooked carrot
¾ cup diced cooked meat (chicken or pork)
1 onion, chopped finely
1 tsp chopped parsley
3 tbsp vegetable oil
1 to 2 tbsp vinegar
salt and pepper to taste
mayonnaise or yogurt to blend

Mix potato, apple, cucumber, carrot, meat, onion and parsley. Add oil, vinegar, salt and pepper. Let stand at least 1 hour. Mix with mayonnaise or yogurt to blend together.
Makes 4 servings.

The first potato recipes were in a book published in Germany in 1581 called Ein New Kochbuch.

Ham 'n Eggs Potato Salad

8 medium potatoes, cooked, peeled and cut in ½-inch cubes
2 tbsp white wine vinegar
1¼ cups mayonnaise
1 tbsp chopped dill
½ tsp dry mustard
pepper to taste
3 cups cooked ham, cut in ½-inch cubes
4 hard-cooked eggs, chopped
1 medium onion, finely chopped
green pepper rings for garnish

While potatoes are still warm, sprinkle with vinegar. Blend mayonnaise, dill, mustard and pepper in large bowl. Add potatoes, mix well and let stand at room temperature for 15 minutes. Stir in ham, eggs and onion. Refrigerate until serving time. Garnish with green pepper rings.
Makes 8 servings.

German Hot Potato Salad

6 cups diced cooked potato
6 slices bacon, cut in small pieces
1 tbsp all-purpose flour
1 tbsp sugar
1 tsp salt
½ tsp dry mustard
⅛ tsp pepper
⅛ tsp paprika
¼ cup water
½ cup vinegar
⅛ tsp celery salt
¼ cup finely chopped onion
¼ cup chopped celery
¼ cup chopped sweet pickle
2 hard-cooked eggs, chopped

Keep potatoes hot. Fry bacon until crisp; remove from pan. Combine flour, sugar, salt, mustard, pepper and paprika and stir into bacon fat. Combine water and vinegar, and gradually add to mixture. Cook until smooth and thickened (about 5 minutes), stirring constantly. Pour over hot potatoes; add remaining ingredients and bacon, and toss lightly until well-mixed.
Makes 6 servings.

German-Style Chilled Potato Salad

Unlike the usual hot potato salads from Germany, this one is chilled well before serving.

5 lbs potatoes, boiled, peeled and sliced
6 slices bacon, diced
½ cup all-purpose flour
4 cups water
6 tbsp granulated sugar
1 tsp salt
⅛ tsp pepper
1 tsp celery salt
¾ cup white vinegar
½ cup chopped onion
6 hard-cooked eggs, sliced

Place cold sliced potatoes in a large bowl. Fry bacon until crisp. Drain, reserving fat. Stir flour into bacon fat and blend well. Gradually add water, stirring constantly until thick. Add sugar, salt, pepper and celery salt. Simmer until thoroughly blended. Add vinegar and bring to a boil. Pour over sliced potatoes; add onion and sliced eggs. Refrigerate to chill through.
Serves 12 to 14.

Dutch Potato Salad

1 cup diced cooked beef
1 dill pickle, minced
1 large apple, peeled and diced
1 cup diced cooked potato
1 small onion, minced
1 tbsp vegetable oil
1½ tbsp vinegar
2 tbsp mayonnaise
2 hard-cooked eggs, sliced, and shredded pickled beets for garnish

Combine beef, pickle, apple, potatoes and onion. Mix together oil, vinegar and mayonnaise; add to meat and potato mixture. Mix well. Put in bowl and garnish with hard-cooked egg slices and pickled beets.
Serves 4.

Danish Potato Salad

Denmark is one of the many countries that combines potatoes with apples. Served with cold baked ham, this salad makes a meal to remember.

¼ cup oil
¼ cup vinegar
1½ cups diced apple
1½ cups diced cooked potato
1 cup diced cooked carrot
1 cup cooked peas (fresh, frozen or canned)
4 hard-boiled eggs, chopped
½ cup chopped onion
½ cup mayonnaise
½ tsp salt
⅛ tsp pepper
radish, celery and/or green pepper, for garnish if desired

Mix oil and vinegar for dressing; combine apple and dressing. Mix well. Add potatoes, carrots, peas, eggs and onion. Mix, then chill for 1 hour. Drain and add mayonnaise. Blend well, adding salt and pepper to taste. Put in bowl and garnish with raw vegetables if desired.
Serves 4.

Polish Potato Salad

6 large potatoes, cooked, peeled and diced
½ cup mayonnaise
½ cup cooked peas
½ cup diced cooked carrots
2 apples, peeled, cored and diced
2 stalks celery, diced
2 dill pickles, chopped finely
1 tbsp freshly chopped parsley
1 tbsp chopped dill
½ cup sour cream
3 tbsp vinegar
1 tsp salt

Mix potatoes with mayonnaise and stand in refrigerator until well-chilled. Combine with remaining ingredients. Mix carefully and chill again before serving.
Makes 6 to 8 servings.

Herring, Beet and Potato Salad

A salad from Finland that really is delicious.

6 medium potatoes, cooked and diced
6 beets, cooked and diced (about 2 cups)
2 apples, peeled and chopped
¼ cup finely chopped onion
1 cup diced pickled herring
½ tsp salt
⅛ tsp pepper
1 cup sour cream
¼ cup mayonnaise
2 to 3 tbsp sugar
1 to 2 tbsp vinegar

Combine potatoes, beets, apples, onion and herring. Sprinkle with salt and pepper. Combine sour cream, mayonnaise, sugar and vinegar. Stir into first mixture. Refrigerate 1½ to 2 hours before serving.
Serves 6.

Carnival Potato Salad

A colourful salad from the United States, sometimes called "Salmagundi."

2 cups diced cooked potato
2 cups diced cooked ham
½ cup chopped celery
½ cup cooked peas
2 hard-cooked eggs, chopped
1 tbsp chopped pimento
2 chopped gherkins
½ to ¾ cup mayonnaise
½ tsp salt
¼ tsp pepper
lettuce, radish and 1 hard-boiled egg, for garnish, if desired

Combine potatoes, ham, celery, peas, eggs, pimento, gherkins, mayonnaise, salt and pepper. Mix well. Put in a lettuce-lined bowl. Garnish with slices of hard-cooked egg and radish roses.
Serves 4.

Soups, Stews and Chowders

Soup can be an appetizer or a main course. It can be served hot or cold and it goes well with everything. How about soup and a sandwich, soup and salad, soup for dinner or soup for lunch? Anytime is soup time.

Soup begins with a good stock. The early settlers had a stock pot on the back of the stove. Each day, soup bones and bits of less-tender meats would go into the stock pot. Small amounts of vegetables and seasonings were added and when the dish had simmered until all the flavour was extracted from the various ingredients, the stock was strained and ready for the next day's soup.

Today we have it much easier, with commercial bouillon cubes and powdered soup bases. For those concerned about msg in commercial bouillon cubes and powdered soup bases, some health food stores carry varieties without added msg. However, whenever possible, I recommend making stock from leftover chicken and turkey, beef ribs and ham. I do occasionally use commercial products to enhance the flavours and I have used them in testing the recipes in this book.

Soups are easy to prepare, nutritious and economical. There's a soup for every occasion, ranging from a clear broth to a chunky chowder.

Potatoes act as carriers and blend well with other ingredients, taking on the colour and absorbing the flavour of whatever they are cooked with.

Most soups and stocks freeze well and actually improve in flavour if made a day early and reheated at serving time.

Potato soup is said to have originated with an American scientist, Benjamin Thompson, in 1795. He wanted to feed the poor, "as well as possible with as little as possible." Potatoes have been used in soup ever since.

153

Cream of Potato Soup

6 medium potatoes, peeled
6 cups water
1 tsp salt
4 slices back bacon,
3 medium onions
1 chicken bouillon cube
2 tbsp soft butter
3 tbsp all-purpose flour
2 cups milk

Combine potatoes, water and salt. Cook until potatoes are tender. Cook and crumble bacon. Stir-fry onion in bacon fat. Add bacon, bouillon cube and butter to soup. Mash well or purée in a blender. Return to heat; mix flour and milk and add to soup. Heat through, but do not boil. *Serves 6.*

Vichyssoise

A creamy potato soup that is equally good served hot or cold. This recipe comes from the P.E.I. Potato Marketing Board.

3 tbsp butter or margarine
4 leeks, finely chopped
1 medium onion, chopped
1 quart chicken stock (may be made with bouillon base)
2 stalks celery, sliced
2 sprigs fresh chopped parsley
2 medium potatoes, peeled and sliced thinly
salt to taste
½ tsp pepper
few drops Worcestershire sauce
pinch curry powder
1 cup heavy cream
2 tbsp chopped chives

Melt butter and add leeks and onion. Cook slowly until vegetables are tender but not brown. Add chicken stock, celery, parsley, potatoes and seasonings. Cook mixture until potatoes are tender. Put soup through a fine sieve or purée in a blender at moderate speed until very smooth. Just before serving, stir 1 cup heavy cream into soup and simmer until heated. Serve hot, or chill and serve ice-cold. Sprinkle with finely chopped chives.
Serves 4 to 6.

Acadian Pea Soup

1 ham bone, with about 2 cups of meat left on
1½ cups dried yellow peas
3 cups diced raw potatoes
1 medium onion, diced
pinch each of thyme, basil and oregano
salt and pepper to taste
1 tbsp parsley flakes

Rinse peas. Place ham bone and peas in a 4-quart soup pot. Add enough cold water to cover ham bone (6 to 8 cups); bring to a boil. Skim off foam. Add potatoes, onion and seasonings. Simmer 3 hours until peas are tender. Sprinkle with parsley. Remove bone from soup. Cut off meat and chop into small pieces. Return meat to soup, heat and serve.
Serves 6 to 8.

Mom's Minestrone

A recipe from my mother's huge collection. An easy-to-prepare minestrone that is extra special.

1½ lbs ground beef
2 cups diced potato
1 cup diced onion
1 cup zucchini
1 cup carrot
1 cup cabbage
½ cup celery
½ cup macaroni
½ cup canned tomato
7 cups water
1 bay leaf
½ tsp thyme
salt to taste
½ tsp pepper
1 tsp Worcestershire sauce
¼ cup parmesan cheese (optional)

Brown meat loosely in fry pan. Add remaining ingredients except for parmesan cheese. Bring to a boil. Lower heat and simmer for 1 to 1½ hours. Sprinkle with parmesan cheese to serve.
Serves 6 to 8.

Cockaleekie (Cock-a-leek-e) Soup

A famous dish from Scotland, this thick soup is served as a main course and eaten with a spoon and fork.

1 boiling fowl or broiler (3 to 3½ lbs) cut in large pieces
½ cup barley
4 cups boiling water
½ cup chopped carrot
½ cup chopped celery
¼ cup chopped onion
salt to taste
¼ tsp white pepper
1 bay leaf
few sprigs fresh chopped parsley
1½ cups thinly sliced leek
½ tsp thyme
1 cup peeled and cubed potato
2 cups milk or light cream

Place the cut-up chicken and barley in a large saucepan and cover with boiling water. Add carrot, celery, onion, salt, pepper, bay leaf and parsley. Cover and let simmer until meat is ready to fall off the bones (1 to 2 hours, depending on the age of the bird). Remove chicken from saucepan and cool until easily handled. Discard bone and skin and chop meat into bite-sized pieces. Skim excess fat from the broth. Add leeks, thyme and potato. Bring to a boil. Reduce heat; cover and simmer for 20 minutes or until barley and potato are tender. Add milk and cut-up chicken. Heat through. Remove and discard bay leaf before serving. *Serves 8.*

Meatless Cabbage-and-Potato Soup

Until researching this book I had never considered combining cabbage and potato in a soup almost "all-their-own." I was surprised to find Cabbage-and-Potato soup is served in several countries, including Ireland and Russia. This recipe is easy to prepare and is very tasty.

3 cups boiling water
4 to 5 chicken bouillon cubes
3 medium potatoes, pared and diced
2 cups shredded cabbage
2 tbsp margarine or butter
1 cup chopped leek or green onion
3 tbsp all-purpose flour
1½ cups milk
2 tsp prepared mustard
½ tsp Worcestershire sauce
¼ tsp pepper
¼ tsp salt
2 drops Tabasco sauce
1½ cups cereal cream

Combine boiling water, bouillon cubes, potatoes and cabbage. Cover and simmer over medium heat until potatoes are tender, about 10 minutes. Sauté leek in melted butter until tender. Stir in flour and cook 2 to 3 minutes. Slowly stir in milk. Add mustard, Worcestershire sauce, pepper, salt and Tabasco sauce. Mix well and stir into broth and vegetable mixture. Slowly stir in cream. Cook over low heat for 15 minutes. Do not boil.
Serves 6 to 8.

Playwright Charles MacArthur taught his daughter Mary what to do when "a person at the dinner table becomes too stuffy": lob a wad of mashed potatoes off the back of a spoon at the victim. He demonstrated the technique on the governess, who was sitting across from him.

Pumpkin-and-Potato Soup

Pumpkin and potato soups are popular in many countries. A friend in Australia sent me several recipes for pumpkin soups. This one is my favourite.

¼ cup butter or margarine
1 medium onion, finely chopped
2 leeks or green onion, chopped
2 medium potatoes, peeled and diced
2 cups cooked pumpkin (canned pumpkin may be used)
2 cups boiling water
2 tbsp chicken bouillon base
salt and pepper to taste
2 cups milk or cream (I use half of each)
chopped fresh parsley or chives for garnish

Sauté onion and leeks in butter until limp, but not brown. Combine with potatoes, pumpkin, water and soup base. Simmer until potatoes are tender. Sieve or put through a blender. Stir in seasonings, milk and cream. Heat slowly. Do not boil. Sprinkle with chives or parsley.
Serves 4 to 6.

Brigitte Van Vliet of Albany, Prince Edward Island, tells how potatoes saved her and her family from starvation:

"*During the last winter of World War II, food and fuel shortages caused untold suffering and death to thousands of people in the western part of Holland, where I lived at the time.*

"*To feed the family, my father tried very hard to supplement the meager food rations. A market gardener and fruit grower, he had never grown potatoes before; yet somehow he managed to obtain a falsified permit to grow spuds. It took him five days to bring the small seed potatoes home by barge. They were stored in a pit in the ground and were covered with straw and clay.*

"*Once a week, we took out seven buckets of spuds, each bucket enough for three meals per day. As the winter progressed, however, the potatoes were disappearing too fast and the rations becoming smaller and smaller. By February, we added sugar beets and crushed tulip bulbs to our diet to stretch the potato supply.*

"*At the end of the war in May, we could only be thankful that our family was saved from starvation by a barge load of potatoes.*"

Mulligan Stew and Dumplings

⅓ cup margarine or butter
⅓ cup all-purpose flour
6 beef bouillon cubes
4 cups boiling water
2 cups diced cooked beef
4 medium onions, sliced
2 large carrots, diced
3 potatoes, diced
½ cup green beans
½ cup fresh or frozen peas
salt and pepper to taste
dash nutmeg

Melt margarine; stir in flour. Dissolve beef cubes in boiling water. Gradually stir into flour and margarine. Cook until it starts to thicken. Add beef, onions, carrots, potatoes, green beans. Bring to a boil and simmer for 30 minutes. Add peas, dumplings and seasonings. Simmer, covered, 15 minutes longer.
Serves 4 to 6.

Dumplings
1 cup all-purpose flour
2 tsp baking powder
2 tbsp margarine, butter or shortening
⅔ cup milk

Mix all ingredients and drop by spoonfuls into hot stew.

Oven Meatball Stew

1 lb ground beef
2 tbsp onion
2 tbsp green pepper
¼ cup cornmeal
1 tsp salt
1½ tsp dry mustard
1 tsp chili powder
1 egg, slightly beaten
½ cup milk
¼ cup all-purpose flour
2 tbsp fat
2 cups tomato juice

4 medium potatoes, cut in large chunks
4 carrots, cut in large pieces
3 medium onions, quartered
salt to taste

Combine ground beef, onion, green pepper, cornmeal, salt, mustard, chili powder, egg and milk. Form into small meatballs. Sprinkle with flour and brown in hot fat. Place in a large casserole. Add remaining flour to frying pan. Blend in tomato juice. Cook until thick. Pour over the meatballs. Arrange vegetables around meat. Add salt to taste. Cover tightly. Bake at 350°F for 1 hour or until vegetables are tender. *Serves 4 to 6.*

Spicy Chuckwagon Stew

A spicy stew with thick chunks of vegetables and beef, this recipe comes from Texas.

2 lbs boneless beef, cut in 1-inch cubes
½ cup all-purpose flour
2½ tsp salt
½ tsp pepper
½ tsp paprika
2 tbsp vegetable oil
1 cup coarsely chopped onion
6 cups water
1 can (20 oz) tomatoes
2 cups thickly sliced carrot
1 cup thickly sliced celery
3 cups potato, cut in 1-inch cubes
1 cup green peas
1 tsp granulated sugar
3 tbsp cornstarch
¼ cup cold water
additional salt and pepper to taste

Coat beef cubes in mixture of flour, salt, pepper and paprika, and brown in vegetable oil. Add onion and brown lightly. Add water, cover and simmer for 30 minutes. Add vegetables and seasonings. Simmer uncovered for 30 minutes or until vegetables are tender. Blend some gravy from the stew into the cornstarch and water mixture and stir into stew until thickened. *Serves 8 to 10.*

After-Class Stew

After a year of hamburgers, canned beans and pizza, our son Mark decided his college cooking would have to improve. When packing his "care package" from home, I enclosed a frozen steak. With one pound of steak, he came up with a recipe to serve six college kids.

1 lb flank steak, cut in thin strips
6 medium potatoes, sliced
3 medium carrots, diagonally sliced (to cook faster)
3 stalks celery, sliced
3 medium onions, sliced
1 cup cubed turnip
2 tbsp oil
¼ tsp garlic salt
3 heaping tsp beef bouillon powder
salt to taste
¼ tsp pepper
1 tbsp soy sauce
1 tsp Worcestershire sauce
3 drops Tabasco sauce
1 can tomato soup
1 cup frozen peas
1 tbsp water
1 tbsp cornstarch

Cut steak and vegetables in thin diagonal slices. Sauté steak in oil until brown. Add all vegetables (except peas), seasonings and soup. Simmer 30 minutes or until vegetables are tender. Stir in frozen peas. Combine cornstarch and water. Add to stew. Cook and stir until thickened and bubbly. Serve with hot biscuits.
Serves 6.

P.E.I. Clam Chowder

3 strips bacon, cut into 1-inch pieces
1 medium onion, chopped
2 tbsp all-purpose flour
1 cup milk
1½ cups light cream
1 cup peeled and cubed potato
1½ cups clam juice
1 cup chopped cooked clams
1 tbsp fresh chopped parsley, or 1 tsp dry parsley

Fry bacon in a 2-quart saucepan over low heat until crisp. Remove and
set aside. Reserve 1½ tbsp bacon fat. Add onion to bacon fat and cook
until transparent. Gradually stir in flour, blending well. Cook 1 minute.
Slowly add milk and cream, stirring constantly until mixture is smooth
and thick. Add bacon. Stir in potatoes and clam juice. Simmer until
potatoes are tender, stirring often (about 15 minutes). Add clams. Simmer until thickened, stirring only to prevent sticking. Sprinkle with
parsley.
Serves 4.

Lobster Chowder

1 lb lobster meat
2 tbsp butter or margarine melted
¾ cup thinly sliced onion
½ cup diced celery
2 cups diced potato
¾ cup diced carrot
3 cups boiling water
salt to taste
⅛ tsp pepper
1 cup evaporated milk

Cut lobster into bite-sized pieces; set aside. In a large saucepan, sauté
onion and celery in butter until limp. Add potato, carrot, water, salt
and pepper. Bring to a boil. Add lobster and cook 10 to 15 minutes. Add
milk. Heat, but do not boil.
Serves 4.

Variations: Any type of white fish may be used with this recipe. I have
tried ling, cod, haddock and canned chicken haddie. All are delicious.

Island Fish Chowder

3 medium potatoes sliced in ¼-inch slices
½ cup diced celery
1½ lbs fish fillets
1 cup cold water
3 slices bacon
2 medium onions, sliced
1 cup boiling water
2½ cups milk
salt to taste
¼ tsp pepper
2 tbsp butter
fresh chopped parsley for garnish

Combine potatoes and celery. Cover with cold water and set aside. Cover fish with 1 cup cold water and heat to simmer for 5 minutes. Strain, reserving liquid. Cut fish in 2-inch pieces. Cut bacon into small pieces and fry in saucepan until crisp. Remove bacon; cook onion slices in bacon fat for 5 minutes. Drain potatoes and celery and add onion slices. Cover with boiling water. Simmer gently until potatoes are tender. Add fish and reserved fish liquid. Cover and simmer for 10 minutes. Add milk, salt, pepper, butter and bacon. To serve, sprinkle with parsley. *Serves 4.*

Seafood Chowder, Manhattan-Style

This main-course chowder can be kept 4 to 5 days in the refrigerator and it also freezes well. Reheating brings out even more flavour.

½ cup chopped bacon
2 medium onions, chopped
2 stalks celery, sliced thinly
3 to 4 medium potatoes, peeled and diced
1 can (28 oz) tomatoes
3 tbsp chicken soup base
3 cups boiling water
1 tbsp chopped fresh parsley, or 1 tsp dry parsley
1 tsp thyme
salt to taste
½ tsp pepper
1 lb white fish, (eg., cod, haddock or ling)
½ lb chopped scallops
1 can (7 oz) shrimp

Sauté bacon. Crumble and set aside. Cook onions and celery in bacon drippings. Add potatoes and cook a few minutes. Add tomatoes, soup base, boiling water, parsley, thyme and seasonings. Cook until potatoes are almost tender. Add white fish and simmer 10 minutes. Add scallops and shrimp and simmer another 6 to 8 minutes. Sprinkle with reserved bacon for garnish when ready to serve.
Serves 6.

Popeye's Fish Chowder

You guessed it—this chowder features spinach along with fish and potatoes.

1 lb fish fillets (any white fish)
½ cup salt pork or bacon, chopped
2 cups diced potatoes
2 stalks celery, chopped
3 tbsp green sliced onion
2 tbsp chicken soup base
2 cups boiling water
3 cups milk
3 tbsp all-purpose flour
1 cup heavy cream
1 can (5 to 6 oz) baby clams, undrained
2 cups finely shredded spinach
salt to taste
¼ tsp pepper
dash of hot pepper sauce, optional

Chop fish coarsely. Cook pork or bacon in a Dutch oven until brown. Drain, reserving 3 tbsp drippings. Add potatoes, celery and onion to drippings. Cook until onion is tender. Add chicken soup base and water. Cover and cook 10 minutes or until potatoes are tender. Add fish and 2½ cups milk. Bring almost to a boil. Reduce heat; simmer until fish is cooked (3 to 5 minutes). Combine remaining cold milk and flour. Blend well. Stir into chowder. Cook and stir until bubbly. Cook one minute longer. Add cream, clams, spinach, salt pork, salt, pepper and hot pepper sauce. Heat through but do not boil.
Serves 8.

Salmon-Vegetable Chowder

One small can of salmon flavours this creamy chowder. Serve with crusty rolls for an economical lunch.

2 medium potatoes, cubed
1 cup water
1 cup milk
1 cup fresh or frozen mixed peas and carrots
1 tbsp butter or margarine
2 tbsp chopped onion
1½ tsp all-purpose flour
1 can (7 oz) salmon (remove bones and flake)
½ tsp Worcestershire sauce
1 tsp lemon juice
salt to taste

Simmer potatoes in water and ¼ cup milk. Sauté onion in butter, stir in flour and add remaining milk to make a cream sauce. Add potatoes and bring close to a boil. Simmer 10 minutes. Add remaining ingredients. Heat but do not boil.
Serves 2 to 4.

New England Turkey Chowder

¾ cup butter or margarine
2 cups diced celery
1 cup chopped onion
8 cups chicken or turkey broth (may be made with bouillon cubes)
2 cups diced cooked turkey
1 can (19 oz) cream-style corn
4 cups cubed cooked potatoes
¾ cup cereal cream
1 tsp ginger
salt and pepper to taste

Sauté onion and celery in butter until transparent. Do not brown. Place broth in large covered kettle. Add remaining ingredients. Stir well. Heat thoroughly for 20 minutes, but do not boil. Season to taste. Serve in heated bowls with crusty rolls.
Serves 8.

Parsnip Chowder

So often parsnips are ignored. Here they combine with potatoes and onion for a delicious chowder.

2 tbsp diced bacon
1 small onion, chopped
2 cups diced parsnips
1 cup diced potatoes
2 cups boiling water
salt to taste
½ tsp pepper
5 cups scalded milk
½ cup butter or margarine
½ cup finely crushed cornflakes
1 tbsp fresh chopped parsley, or 1 tsp dry parsley

Sauté bacon. Add onion and cook until tender. Add vegetables, seasonings and water. Simmer until vegetables are tender. Stir in remaining ingredients and cook until chowder is almost to the boiling point. Do not boil after milk is added.
Serves 6.

Corn Chowder

4 slices bacon, cut in small pieces
½ cup chopped onion
2 cups diced potato
1 cup boiling water
salt to taste
⅛ tsp pepper
1 tbsp all-purpose flour
2 cups 2% evaporated milk
1 can (19 oz) cream-style corn

Fry bacon until crisp; remove from pan and drain. Sauté onion in bacon fat. Drain off excess fat. Add potatoes, water and seasonings. Cover and simmer about 10 minutes. Combine flour and milk. Add the vegetables. Stir until smooth and thick. Add corn and heat through. Sprinkle with bacon just before serving.
Serves 4.

Baked Potatoes

One of the most popular items in today's fast-food industry is the baked potato. Served with a variety of toppings, a baked potato is a quick nutritious snack, without an abundance of calories. In this section you will find a selection of easy-to-prepare potato toppings that you can make at home.

Another easy way to jazz up an old favourite is to stuff a baked potato. Included are several recipes for stuffings that will make baked potatoes a special treat.

Baked Potatoes

Select medium baking potatoes of uniform size. Scrub thoroughly with a vegetable brush. If desired, rub skins with oil to enhance flavour and appearance. Puncture skin in several places with a fork to prevent potatoes from exploding in the oven. Do not wrap in foil as this gives you soggy, steamed potatoes. Bake in hot oven (400°F) 45 to 60 minutes. After removing from oven, make a crosswise cut in each potato and pinch to let steam escape. If serving with the traditional butter, salt and pepper, spread butter in the cuts on top of each potato and serve at once.

Classy Baked Potatoes

Combining dairy foods with potato supplements the protein of the potato. Try 1 cup of the following dairy food bases:

sour cream
cottage cheese and lemon juice, blended
mayonnaise
yogurt **or**
cheese sauce seasoned with thyme, rosemary, paprika or dry mustard

To this base add ¼ to ½ cup of one or a combination of the following ingredients:

green onion	radish
chives	crisp bacon
fresh parsley	ham
celery	chicken **or**
cucumber	sautéed mushrooms

Makes enough for 4 to 6 potatoes.

Sour Cream and Chives

1 cup sour cream
3 tbsp minced chives
2 tbsp minced parsley

Combine all ingredients and serve over hot baked potatoes.
Serves 6.

Mock Sour Cream

Cut calories with this delicious substitute.

½ cup water
1 tbsp lemon juice
1 cup creamed cottage cheese
½ tsp salt

Combine all ingredients in blender and purée at high speed until completely smooth (about 10 seconds), or beat with an electric mixer. Spoon onto hot baked potatoes as desired.
Serves 6 to 8.

Lobster Topping

Dress up a baked potato with this creamy lobster topping.

1 cup canned diced lobster meat
1 pkg (4 oz) cream cheese
½ cup mayonnaise
¼ cup sour cream
2 tbsp lobster juice
2 tsp lemon juice
½ clove garlic, crushed
1 tsp chives or parsley

Beat together cream cheese, mayonnaise and sour cream. Add lobster juice, lemon juice, garlic and chives. Beat well. Stir in lobster. Serve over hot baked potatoes.
Serves 6 to 8.

Yogurt Topping

½ cup plain yogurt
1 to 2 tbsp chopped sweet pickle
½ tsp sugar
2 tbsp chopped onion
dash pepper
dash celery salt
½ tsp lemon juice

Combine all ingredients and chill. Serve on hot baked potatoes.
Serves 4 to 6.

Bacon-Dill Topping

4 slices bacon
¼ cup chopped dill pickle
¼ cup melted butter or margarine

Fry bacon until crisp. Drain on paper towels and crumble. Mix with pickle and butter. Serve over hot baked potatoes.
Serves 6.

Chili Cheddar Topper

1 medium chopped onion
¼ cup chopped green pepper
1 clove garlic, minced
2 tbsp butter or margarine
1 lb ground beef
1 tbsp chili powder
¼ tsp thyme
1 tsp marjoram
1 can (15 oz) tomato sauce
2 tbsp ketchup
⅛ tsp cayenne pepper
shredded cheddar cheese

Sauté onion, green pepper and garlic in butter for 5 minutes; add ground beef and cook another 5 minutes. Drain excess fat. Stir in chili powder, thyme and marjoram; cook 3 minutes. Add tomato sauce, ketchup and cayenne pepper seasoning. Cover and simmer until cooked through. Serve over baked potatoes; sprinkle with shredded cheddar cheese.
Serves 6 to 8.

Italian Topping

1 tsp butter
2 tbsp chopped onion
1 tbsp chopped fresh parsley
¼ tsp salt or celery salt
½ tsp oregano
¼ tsp basil
dash pepper
1 cup diced tomato

Sauté onions in butter until transparent. Add remaining ingredients. Simmer 10 minutes. Keep warm until potatoes are cooked.
Serves 4 to 6.

Photos for stuffed baked potatoes are often taken with raw potatoes. Baked potatoes are tasty, but definitely not photogenic.

Hamburger Stroganoff Topper

1 medium chopped onion
¼ lb sliced mushrooms
2 tbsp butter or margarine
¾ lb hamburger
1 tsp paprika
1 tsp prepared mustard
½ cup beef broth
½ tsp salt
¼ tsp pepper
1¼ cups sour cream

Sauté onion and mushrooms in butter; add hamburger and cook until pinkness leaves meat. Drain excess fat. Stir in paprika, prepared mustard, beef broth, salt and pepper. Simmer until well-blended. Just before serving, stir in sour cream and heat to serving temperature. Do not boil. Serve over hot baked potatoes.
Serves 6 to 8.

Chinese-Style Baked Potatoes

1 lb sliced mushrooms
½ cup sliced green pepper
½ cup chopped onion
1 clove garlic, minced
¼ cup vegetable oil
2 tomatoes, chopped
1 can (8 oz) whole kernel corn, drained
1 tbsp soy sauce
1 tbsp vegetable oil
½ tsp sugar
1 tsp grated ginger root

Stir fry mushrooms, green pepper, onion and garlic in oil until crispy-tender. Add tomatoes and corn, and stir fry 3 minutes longer. Add soy sauce, oil, sugar and ginger root. Heat through. Cut baked potatoes almost in half, lengthwise; fluff with a fork and top with vegetable mixture.
Serves 6.

Stuffed Baked Potatoes

Bake medium-sized potatoes at 400°F 45 to 60 minutes. Cut potato open. Scoop out insides; mash. Add hot milk, butter and seasonings. Beat until fluffy; pile lightly into potato shells, return to oven and brown.

Some ideas for seasonings (amounts are for 1 potato):
3 tbsp grated cheese
1 tbsp diced onion
¼ cup cooked meat with 1 tsp diced onion
2 tbsp crisp bacon bits
1 tsp chopped chives or parsley flakes
¼ cup salmon with 2 tbsp cooked peas

Twice-Baked Cheese-Stuffed Potatoes

4 medium baked potatoes
1½ cups shredded gouda cheese
½ cup sour cream
2 tbsp butter or margarine
2 tbsp finely chopped green onion
1 tbsp fresh chopped parsley
1 tbsp horseradish (optional)
¾ tsp salt
4 slices bacon, cooked to crisp and crumbled

Cut baked potatoes in half, lengthwise. Scoop out centre and mash with 1 cup cheese, sour cream, butter, onion, parsley, horse radish and salt. Mix well. Fill potato shells with mixture; sprinkle with remaining cheese. Bake at 350°F for 20 minutes. Sprinkle bacon over potatoes for last few minutes of baking.
Serves 4.

Reuben Spuds

¼ cup corned beef, cut in thin strips
½ cup drained sauerkraut
¼ cup shredded Swiss cheese

Preheat oven to 350°F. Split baked potato almost in half lengthwise. Fluff potato with fork. Top with corned beef, sauerkraut and cheese. Bake until cheese melts, about 10 minutes. Serve with mustard if desired.
Serves 1.

Low-Calorie Stuffed Baked Potatoes

4 medium baked potatoes
⅔ cup skim milk
1 cup cottage cheese
salt
pepper
paprika

Preheat oven to 400°F. Cut baked potatoes in half, lengthwise. Scoop out potato and mash well with milk, cottage cheese, and salt and pepper to taste. Spoon into potato shells; sprinkle with paprika and bake until lightly browned.
Serves 8. Approximately 75 calories per serving.

Crab-Stuffed Baked Potatoes

Rock crabs are abundant in most fishing areas of Prince Edward Island. In recent years crab fishing has become an important industry. This delicious recipe using rock crab with potatoes comes from the P.E.I. Department of Fisheries.

6 baked potatoes
1 tbsp softened butter or margarine
¾ cup sour cream
1 small onion, grated
¼ tsp cayenne pepper
6 oz fresh rock crab meat (cartilage removed)
¼ cup diced mushroom
½ cup grated cheddar cheese

Preheat oven to 375°F. Cut baked potatoes in half lengthwise and carefully scoop out insides, reserving the skins. In a medium bowl combine potato, butter, sour cream, onion and cayenne pepper. Mash with a potato masher until smooth. Fold in crab meat and diced mushrooms. Spoon mixture into the 12 potato halves. Sprinkle with grated cheese and place on a baking sheet. Bake 10 to 15 minutes until hot. Serve at once.
Serves 6.

The first toy advertised on American television is said to have been "Mr. Potato Head."

Lobster Stuffed Baked Potatoes

Prince Edward Island lobster and potatoes—a perfect combination.

½ cup diced cooked lobster meat
6 baked potatoes
1 tbsp butter or margarine
½ cup sour cream
¼ cup grated onion
¼ tsp pepper
¼ cup diced mushrooms
½ cup grated cheddar cheese

Preheat oven to 375°F. Cut baked potatoes in half lengthwise and carefully scoop out insides, reserving the skins. In a bowl, mash the potato,
then add butter, sour cream, onion and pepper. Beat until smooth. Fold
in lobster meat and mushrooms, and place mixture back in the potato
skin halves. Sprinkle with grated cheese and place on a baking sheet.
Bake 15 to 20 minutes, or until potatoes are heated through.
Serves 6.

Sausage-Stuffed Baked Potatoes

8 large baked potatoes
1 cup scalded light cream
⅓ cup melted butter or margarine
2 tsp salt
¼ tsp pepper
8 pork sausages, cooked
2 tsp minced fresh parsley
½ tsp Worcestershire sauce
paprika

Preheat oven to 400°F. Cut tops of potatoes lengthwise. Scoop out pulp
and mash with cream, butter, salt and pepper until fluffy. Fill potato
shells half-full with this mixture; put in a cooked sausage and sprinkle
with parsley and a few drops of Worcestershire sauce. Cover with remaining potato mixture. Sprinkle with paprika and bake until heated
through and brown on top (about 15 minutes).
Serves 8.

Salmon-Stuffed Baked Potatoes

The P.E.I. Department of Fisheries developed this recipe.

6 baked potatoes
½ cup hot milk
1 tsp salt
¼ tsp pepper
¼ tsp thyme
1 egg, beaten
2 (7 oz) cans pink salmon
¼ cup finely chopped onion
1 tbsp parsley flakes
½ cup fine dry bread crumbs
¼ cup melted butter or margarine

Cut potatoes in half lengthwise while hot. Scoop insides of potatoes into a bowl, keeping shells intact. Set shells on a large baking pan. Add hot milk to potato and beat or mash until light and fluffy. Add salt, pepper, thyme and egg, and blend well. Drain salmon and flake. Fold salmon, onion and parsley into potato mixture. Spoon mixture into the potato shells. Combine bread crumbs and butter and sprinkle over potato. Bake at 400°F for about 20 minutes or until browned and heated through.
Serves 6.

Accompaniments

Accompaniments are the "little extras" that demonstrate flair. Try potato pancakes for Sunday brunch or as a side dish with steak, roast, ham or barbecued meats. How about some home fries for a country-style harvest-time breakfast? Crispy fries and creamy casseroles that mix well with other vegetables, as well as many exciting new ideas, are found in this section.

Quick Potato Accompaniments

Sausage Potatoes
Remove centres from baking potatoes with an apple corer. Insert part of a sausage into each potato. Bake in a cake pan, basting from time to time with the fat that drips from the sausage.

Julienne or Shoestring Potatoes
Peel potatoes. Cut in thin strips (¼ x ¼ x 2 inches). Soak in ice water for 45 minutes. Drain. Dry between towels. Deep fry in fat at 325°F until brown. Drain on brown paper or paper towels.

Home-made Potato Chips
Peel potatoes. Slice thinly; cover with ice water and let stand for 45 minutes. Drain. Dry on towels. Deep fry in fat at 325°F until golden brown. Drain on brown paper. Sprinkle with salt.

Potatoes Lyonnaise
Potatoes Lyonnaise is a fancy name for fried potatoes. Simply sauté onion in fat, add diced cooked potatoes and fry until browned on the bottom and well heated through. Sprinkle with salt and pepper.

Potatoes Persillade (Parsley Potatoes)
Add ½ cup lemon juice to ½ cup melted butter or margarine. Pour over whole new cooked potatoes. Sprinkle with fresh chopped parsley.

French-Fried Potatoes
Cut peeled or unpeeled potatoes into sticks ¼ to ½ inch thick. Soak for 45 minutes in ice water. Drain and dry thoroughly. Deep fry in hot fat at 370°F for 5 to 7 minutes. Drain on absorbent paper. Sprinkle with salt. Do not put too many potatoes in the serving dish at once or French fries will become soggy.

Roast Potatoes
Peel and quarter medium-sized potatoes. Parboil for 8 to 10 minutes. Put in a pan with a roast about 45 minutes before the meat is done. Baste with meat juices. Save the water from parboiling the potatoes to use in gravy or other recipes.

Flemish Hash
Rice or sieve hot boiled potatoes. To each cup of potatoes add ½ cup buttermilk, 1 tbsp butter or margarine and salt and pepper to taste. Beat thoroughly until light and fluffy. Serve with any meat or fish dinner.

Quick Croquettes
Season leftover mashed potatoes with salt and pepper. Add one tsp butter or margarine for each cup of potatoes. Form into patties. Coat with Shake 'N Bake, bread crumbs, crushed cornflakes or flour and seasonings. Bake until crispy in a moderate oven (350°F) for 15 to 20 minutes.

Hash Browns

Today's "hash browns" were yesterday's ordinary fried potatoes—the only difference is the addition of a few onion slices. These were served almost nightly on P.E.I.

One of my best memories is the smell of fresh baked bread and fried potatoes when I arrived home from school.

2 tbsp fat (butter or margarine, bacon drippings or vegetable oil)
2 cups cubed cold boiled potato
1 tbsp parsley flakes
½ tsp salt
dash pepper
finely chopped onion

Melt fat in a heavy frying pan. Add other ingredients. Mix well, fry until browned.
Serves 2.

Barbecued Potatoes and Carrots

Enjoy barbecued flavour year-round with this oven-baked recipe.

4 cups thinly sliced potatoes, peeled or unpeeled
1 cup carrot, sliced diagonally to speed cooking
½ cup chopped celery
½ cup chopped onion
½ cup shredded cheese of your choice
3 tbsp all-purpose flour
salt and pepper to taste
⅓ cup ketchup
⅛ tsp cayenne pepper
1 tsp Worcestershire sauce
½ tsp garlic salt
2 cups milk

Preheat oven to 375°F. Combine potatoes, carrots, celery, onion and cheese. Add flour, salt and pepper and mix well. Put in greased casserole. Combine remaining ingredients and pour over vegetable mixture. Cover and bake for 1 hour. Stir. Bake uncovered until cooked through and browned on top.
Serves 4 to 6.

Potato Knishes

Knishes originated in Israel. Popular now throughout many parts of the world, they were introduced to me by Cindy Chase of Halifax, Nova Scotia. This recipe was first published in Peru in the C.I.P. Women's Club Cookbook.

Dough
6 cups all-purpose flour
1 tsp baking soda
1 egg
1 egg white
1½ cups lukewarm water
¾ cup vegetable oil

Filling
12 medium potatoes (about 4 lbs), cooked and mashed
1½ cups chopped onion
¼ cup vegetable oil
2 beaten eggs
salt and pepper to taste

Dough: Combine flour and soda. Make a hole in the centre and add beaten egg and egg whites and ¼ cup of water. Gradually mix with a knife, working from the inside out and adding more water in small amounts (about ¼ cup at a time). When well-mixed, divide into 6 balls. Knead with your hands and throw dough on counter top several times. With a small amount of flour, add 1 tbsp of oil to each roll. Knead until smooth and elastic enough for a thumb print to stay for a few seconds in the dough. Place dough in a pie plate and pour remaining oil over balls to soak. Let stand at least 1 hour before using.

Filling: Sauté onions in vegetable oil. Mix potatoes with onions, eggs, salt and pepper.

To assemble Knishes, roll dough with a rolling pin; press with hands until very thin. Holding dough in your hands above a table, begin stretching in the middle and working towards the outside. Each ball of dough should be as thin as paper (about 1/16 of an inch). Form potato mixture into a long slender roll, about 1 inch in diameter. Roll dough around potato mixture. Seal. Preheat oven to 400°F. Cut rolls into 1½-inch pieces. Push ends partially shut and place ends down on a shallow greased baking sheet. Bake 45 minutes in a 400°F oven, until lightly browned.
Makes 12 knishes.

Scalloped Potatoes

6 medium potatoes, peeled and thinly sliced
1 medium onion, sliced
2 tbsp all-purpose flour
1 tsp salt
pepper to taste
2 cups hot milk
2 tbsp butter or margarine

Preheat oven to 350°F. Layer sliced potatoes and onion in casserole. Sprinkle flour, salt and pepper over layers. Cover with hot milk and dot with butter. Bake 1 hour covered. Remove cover for last 15 minutes of cooking time.
Serves 4 to 6.

Celery-Cheese Potato Scallop

This can be made ahead and frozen. Thaw before reheating.

2 tbsp onion
2 tbsp celery leaves
few sprigs fresh chopped parsley
1½ tbsp all-purpose flour
2 tbsp butter or margarine
¾ tsp salt
⅛ tsp pepper
¾ cup milk
3 medium potatoes, peeled and sliced
1 cup grated cheddar cheese
dash paprika

Blend onion, celery, parsley, flour, butter, salt, pepper and milk in a blender. Arrange potato slices in a buttered 1-quart casserole. Pour blended mixture over potatoes. Sprinkle with cheese and paprika. Bake 350°F degrees for 1 hour.
Serves 4.

Gangster John Dillinger is reported to have carved a pistol from a potato. He dyed it with iodine, which facilitated his escape from prison.

Whipped Cream Potatoes

Serve with steak, fried chicken or baked ham—mashed potatoes that are out of this world!

8 medium potatoes, boiled and mashed
1 tsp salt
1 pint whipping cream
½ lb grated cheddar cheese

Combine mashed potatoes and ½ pint of whipping cream. Beat at medium speed with electric mixer until thick and creamy. Add salt and pepper to taste and sprinkle with half the grated cheese. Stir lightly. Put in a large baking dish. Whip remaining ½ pint of cream. Spread over potato mixture. Sprinkle with remaining cheese. Bake uncovered at 300°F for 1 to 1½ hours.
Serves 8 to 10.

Spinach and Potato Casserole

Double this recipe and freeze half for later. Swiss chard may be used instead of spinach.

4 to 5 medium potatoes, cooked and mashed
⅓ cup sour cream
1 tsp salt
dash pepper
½ tsp granulated sugar
½ cup butter or margarine
¼ to ½ cup milk
2 tsp chopped chives
⅛ tsp dill seed
1 cup cooked well-drained spinach
½ cup grated cheddar cheese

Preheat oven to 400°F. Combine potatoes, sour cream, salt, pepper, sugar and butter. Add enough milk to make a fluffy mixture. Stir in chives, dill seed and chopped spinach. Put in a greased casserole. Sprinkle with cheese. Bake 20 minutes.
Serves 4 to 6.

Potato Dumplings

6 medium potatoes, boiled and mashed well
1 tsp salt
½ tsp pepper
2 tbsp melted shortening
1 tsp nutmeg
4 eggs, beaten
2 tbsp all-purpose flour
2 tbsp bread crumbs

Combine all ingredients and beat thoroughly. Drop by spoonfuls into salted boiling water. Cover tightly and boil about 12 minutes.
Yields 20 dumplings.

Potato Cheese Dumplings

This recipe from Jamaica is served with sausages. Unlike most dumpling recipes, it is not boiled.

3 lbs potatoes, mashed (8 to 9 medium potatoes)
¼ cup butter
3 tbsp milk
½ tsp salt
¼ tsp pepper
¾ cup grated cheddar cheese
paprika

Preheat oven to 375°F. Combine potatoes, butter, milk, salt and pepper. Form into balls. Roll in grated cheese. Bake in a well-buttered pan or casserole dish for about 20 minutes.
Serves 8.

On her way down to the local pond where my mother-in-law as a child went ice skating, she would carry baked potatoes in her skates. When she arrived at the pond, she had warm skates to wear. She put the same potatoes in her boots to ensure cozy feet on the long walk home.

Potato Soufflé

Soufflés are not as difficult to make as many believe. Surprise your guests with this light and tasty version.

3 cups hot mashed potato
2 tbsp butter
2 tbsp chopped onion
1 tsp salt
2 tsp chopped parsley
shake of cayenne pepper (optional)
3 eggs, separated

Preheat oven to 350°F. Combine potato, butter, onion, salt, parsley and cayenne pepper; mix thoroughly. Beat egg whites until stiff. Beat egg yolks and add to potato mixture. Gently fold in egg whites. Put in a greased soufflé dish. Set in a pan of water. Bake 1 hour.
Serves 4.

Potatoes Alaska

Also called "Snow-capped Potatoes," these tiny potato "mountains" are made with mashed potato.

4 medium potatoes, cooked and mashed
2 tbsp butter or margarine
2 egg yolks
2 tbsp chopped green onion tops or chives
½ tsp salt
dash pepper
2 egg whites
2 tbsp mayonnaise
½ tsp lemon juice

Preheat oven to 350°F. Combine potatoes, butter, egg yolks, green onion, salt and pepper. Mix well. Using an ice cream scoop, make mounds of potatoes on a foil-covered baking sheet. Beat egg whites until stiff peaks form; fold in mayonnaise and lemon juice. Top each potato mound with a spoonful of egg-white mixture. Bake for 10 to 12 minutes.
Serves 6 to 8.

Swiss-Parmesan Potato Casserole

1¼ cups grated parmesan cheese
½ tsp salt
⅛ tsp pepper
¼ tsp nutmeg
6 potatoes, peeled and thinly sliced
6 tbsp butter
½ cup cream
½ cup grated Swiss cheese
2 tbsp chopped chives

Preheat oven to 400°F. Mix together parmesan cheese, salt, pepper and nutmeg. Layer potatoes in a buttered 2-quart casserole dish, sprinkling each layer with the cheese mixture. Dot with butter and cover tightly; bake for 1 hour. Uncover and pour cream over the top. Sprinkle with Swiss cheese. Bake uncovered for 5 minutes until cheese melts. Sprinkle with chives before serving.
Serves 6.

Duchess Potatoes

Try this recipe at your next dinner party. Serve with a roast or with baked stuffed salmon.

3 cups hot riced potato
2 tbsp butter
1 tsp salt
few grains paprika
3 egg yolks, beaten
1 egg yolk, beaten with 1 tbsp cold water

Preheat oven to 350°F. Combine potato, butter, salt, paprika and egg yolks. Use a pastry bag to form rosettes or pyramids in a baking dish. Brush with egg yolk-water mixture. Bake for 15 minutes.

Variation: Duchess Potatoes make a nice topping for casseroles or meat loaf.

Potatoes provide more edible matter than the combined worldwide consumption of milk, meat, poultry and seafood.

Sugar-Browned Potatoes

An excellent recipe when made with Sebago potatoes, although any small, smooth, evenly formed potato works well.

1 lb small potatoes
salted water
2 tbsp granulated sugar
¼ cup melted butter or margarine

Cook potatoes until just tender in salted water. Drain. Cool slightly. Combine sugar and butter in a skillet. Add potatoes and heat, stirring frequently until potatoes are evenly browned and glazed.
Serves 4.

Roadside Potatoes

I have often wondered where this recipe got its name!

1 large onion, cut in chunks
1½ tsp all-purpose flour
2 tsp salt
few drops Tabasco sauce
1 cup milk
4 medium potatoes, peeled
1 cup grated cheddar cheese

Preheat oven to 350°F. Grease an 8-inch square cake pan. Put onion, flour, salt, Tabasco sauce and milk in a blender. Purée until completely blended. Grate potatoes and cheese into milk mixture. Pour into prepared pan. Bake 1 hour or until cooked through and golden on top.
Serves 4.

Basque Potatoes

This recipe can be prepared in an electric frying pan. Nice for summer menus when you don't want to heat the kitchen by using the oven.

1 medium onion, sliced
1 clove garlic
2 tbsp vegetable oil
¾ cup fresh chopped parsley
¼ cup pimento

⅛ tsp pepper
1 chicken bouillon cube
1 cup hot water
6 to 8 medium potatoes, peeled and thinly sliced

Sauté onion and garlic in vegetable oil. Remove and discard garlic. Layer thinly sliced potatoes and onion in skillet. Combine other ingredients and pour over potatoes. Heat to boiling. Cover and simmer until potatoes are tender, about 20 minutes.
Serves 6 to 8.

Ooh-La-La Potatoes

This recipe from France is best if made a day ahead and reheated.

6 medium potatoes, cooked, peeled and cubed
1 cup shredded cheddar cheese
6 tbsp butter or margarine
¾ cup sour cream
3 green onions, chopped
1 tsp salt
¼ tsp pepper

Preheat oven to 300°F. Melt cheese and butter. Combine with remaining ingredients. Bake in a greased 2-quart casserole dish for 25 minutes.
Serves 6.

Potato Phili

This casserole can be made ahead and frozen. Thaw before baking.

8 medium potatoes, cooked and mashed
4 ounces cream cheese
½ cup plain yogurt
1 tbsp onion salt
⅛ tsp pepper
1 tbsp butter

Preheat oven to 350°F. Stir ingredients into mashed potatoes and put in a greased casserole dish. Dot with butter. Bake covered for 30 minutes. If freezing, cover tightly with plastic wrap. Cool in refrigerator and then place in freezer. Thaw before baking.
Serves 8.

Potatoes Hollandaise

3 cups sliced raw potato
enough chicken broth to cover
⅓ cup butter or margarine
1 tbsp lemon juice
salt to taste
1½ tsp finely chopped parsley

Cook potatoes in stock. Drain. Cream butter, lemon juice and salt. Add to potatoes and cook 3 minutes. Sprinkle with parsley. (Discard chicken stock or use in soup or gravy.)
Serves 4.

O'Brien Potatoes

Two cups diced cooked meat or fish may be added for a variation of this Irish recipe.

4½ cups diced cooked potato
1 cup chopped onion
½ cup chopped celery
¾ tsp salt
dash pepper
¼ cup fresh chopped parsley
¼ cup oil

Combine potato, onion, celery, salt, pepper and parsley. Fry in fat until slightly browned and thoroughly heated.
Serves 4 to 6.

Spanish Potatoes

¼ cup butter or margarine
¼ cup chopped onion
2 tbsp chopped green pepper
2 tbsp chopped pimento
4 cups boiled potatoes (use small whole potatoes or diced potatoes)
salt and pepper to taste

Sauté onion, pepper and pimento in butter. Add drained potatoes and cook until brown. Season with salt and pepper.
Serves 6.

Chantilly Potatoes

3 cups mashed potato
½ cup grated cheddar cheese
½ cup stiffly beaten heavy cream

Preheat oven to 325°F. Pile mashed potatoes in a baking dish. Spread cream over potatoes and sprinkle with cheese. Bake until delicately browned, 20 to 30 minutes.
Serves 6.

Drunken Potatoes

Make these in advance and put in the oven at the last minute.

6 medium baking potatoes, peeled and sliced thinly
½ cup vermouth
¼ cup butter or margarine
salt and pepper to taste

Preheat oven to 375°F. Arrange potatoes in greased pie plate, overlapping the slices. Pour vermouth over potatoes and sprinkle with seasonings. Dot with butter. Bake uncovered until tender, 30 to 40 minutes.
Serves 6.

Twenty pounds of potatoes can grow a ton of food in one year.

China in 1984 grew 12.5 million acres of potatoes.

Potatoes occupy approximately 50 billion acres of land worldwide.

The potato grows from below sea level in the Netherlands to altitudes of 14,000 feet in the Himalayas and Andes mountain regions.

Potatoes are grown in the deserts of Australia and Africa.

Potatoes have been grown on Ellesmere Island, north of the Arctic Circle.

Chicken Curried Potatoes

Chicken stock and a light taste of curry powder add an eastern taste to potatoes. Serve with roast chicken.

4 tbsp butter
¼ cup finely chopped onion
3 cups cold cooked potato cubes
⅔ cup chicken stock (may be made with bouillon powder)
1 tsp curry powder
1½ tsp lemon juice
salt and pepper to taste

Sauté onion in butter until limp. Do not brown. Add potatoes and cook until butter is absorbed. Add chicken stock and seasonings. Cook until liquid is absorbed into the mixture.
Serves 4.

Cheddar-Cheese Scalloped Potatoes

This easily prepared version of an old favourite can be made ahead, frozen and reheated.

6 medium potatoes, peeled and sliced
¼ cup sliced onion
¼ cup chopped celery
3 tbsp all-purpose flour
¼ cup butter
1½ tsp salt
¼ tsp pepper
1½ cups milk
1 cup grated cheddar cheese
dash paprika

Preheat oven to 350°F. Arrange potato slices in a greased 2-quart casserole dish. Combine onion, celery, flour, butter, salt and pepper in a blender. Pour in milk and blend for 30 seconds. Pour mixture over potato slices; sprinkle with cheese and paprika. Bake for 45 to 55 minutes.
Serves 6 to 8.

Dutch Potato Casserole

6 medium potatoes, boiled and sliced thinly
2 tbsp chopped onion
1 tbsp fresh chopped parsley
½ tsp salt
¼ tsp pepper
1 egg, beaten
½ cup milk
1 cup bread crumbs, stirred with 2 tbsp melted butter

Preheat oven to 350°F. Layer potatoes, onions and seasonings in a casserole dish. Combine egg and milk. Pour over potatoes. Cover with bread crumbs. Bake for 30 minutes.
Serves 4.

Golden Fleck Casserole

Carrots combine with potatoes to make a colourful and easy casserole. Serve with cold meats for luncheon meals or with any roasts, steaks or chops for a full-course dinner.

4 medium potatoes, peeled and sliced
4 medium carrots, peeled and sliced
1 medium onion, sliced thinly
2 tbsp butter
1 can (10 oz) cream of mushroom soup
1 soup can water

In a greased casserole, layer potatoes, carrots and onions. Dot with butter. Pour soup and water over the layers. Cover. Bake at 350°F for 35 minutes. Uncover and bake 20 minutes longer or until vegetables are tender.
Serves 4.

The Dutch potato industry is now worth more than the tulip industry. About one-quarter of Dutch farmland is used for potatoes.

Cheese-Creamed Potatoes

This recipe, from the kitchen of Peggy Drummond, Freetown, P.E.I., is a great way to use up leftover cold potatoes. Serve with baked ham and a green vegetable.

3 cups sliced cold potato
2 tbsp butter
2 tbsp all-purpose flour
1½ cups milk
1 cup grated cheese
½ tsp salt
⅛ tsp pepper

Preheat oven to 400°F. Place potatoes in a greased casserole dish. Melt butter in a saucepan. Stir in flour and gradually add milk, grated cheese and seasonings. Stir over medium heat until thoroughly blended and thickened. Pour over potatoes. Bake until bubbly and browned on top, about 30 minutes.
Serves 4.

Potatoes Almondine

A company recipe that is excellent with roast meats. This casserole can be made a day ahead, refrigerated and reheated.

4 medium potatoes, cooked and mashed
1½ cups cottage cheese
¼ cup sour cream
2 tbsp chopped green onion
1½ tsp salt
¼ tsp pepper
2 tbsp melted butter
¼ cup slivered almonds

Preheat oven to 350°F. Combine mashed potatoes, cottage cheese, sour cream, onion, salt and pepper. Beat with electric mixer until smooth. Put in a shallow buttered casserole dish. Sprinkle with almonds and brush with melted butter. Bake for 30 minutes.
Serves 6 to 8.

Potato Puff (Microwave)

This airy creation is tasty and easy to prepare.

2 cups hot, mashed potato*
2 eggs, separated
1 cup milk
2 tbsp softened butter
2 tsp grated onion
1 tbsp dried parsley flakes
½ tsp salt
dash of pepper
½ cup grated cheddar cheese
paprika

Beat egg whites until stiff. Blend egg yolks, milk, butter, onion and seasonings; add to mashed potatoes and mix until well-blended. Fold in beaten egg whites and grated cheese. Gently spoon into a buttered 2-quart casserole. Sprinkle with paprika. Place casserole on inverted plate in microwave. Microwave on high 10 to 12 minutes, rotating dish every 5 minutes.

*Tip — for added convenience, use leftover mashed potatoes, reheated in the microwave 2 minutes on high.
Serves 4.

Second-Day Potatoes (Microwave)

An excellent use for leftover potatoes.

4 medium cooked potatoes, unpeeled
¼ tsp salt
1 tbsp dried parsley
½ tsp marjoram
¼ cup finely chopped onion
1½ cup grated cheddar cheese
¼ cup melted butter

Slice unpeeled potatoes. Arrange in a 1-quart casserole. In a bowl, blend salt, parsley, marjoram, onion and cheese. Drizzle butter evenly over potatoes. Sprinkle with cheese mixture. Microwave on high for 3 to 5 minutes, rotating halfway through cooking time.
Makes 4 to 6 servings.

Potato-Cheese Bake

This delicious recipe comes from the kitchen of Erma Hickey, of Sherwood Farm Tourist Home at Darnley, P.E.I. Erma tells me she serves this often to her guests along with baked ham and hot curried fruit.

7 to 8 medium potatoes, cooked, peeled and cubed **or**
1 pkg frozen hash browns
1 can (10½ oz) cream of chicken soup
1 cup chopped onion
2 cups sour cream
2 cups grated cheddar cheese

Preheat oven to 350°F. Combine all ingredients. Place in a large greased casserole dish. Bake until browned on top and heated through.
Serves 8.

Hot Curried Fruit
2 cups fresh or canned peaches
2 cups fresh or canned pears
2 cups fresh or canned apricots
2 cups fresh or canned pineapple
2 tbsp butter
¼ cup brown sugar
1½ tsp curry powder
1 can (16 oz) dark bing cherries

Combine fruits (if using canned fruit, drain well). Stir in butter, brown sugar and curry powder. Heat in 350°F oven. (This can be made at the last minute and popped into a microwave for 3 to 4 minutes.) Just before serving, stir in drained cherries.

** Fruits may be substituted to suit individual taste.

Sea captains and sailors ate potatoes for prevention of scurvy. One medium potato contains about 35 per cent of an adult's daily requirement of Vitamin C.

Colcannon

A traditional Irish dish, no potato cookbook would be complete without a recipe for this creamy specialty.

3 to 4 medium potatoes, peeled and cut in quarters
2 tbsp milk or light cream
¼ tsp salt
⅛ tsp pepper
2 cups chopped cabbage
2 tbsp butter or margarine
¼ cup chopped onion
2 tbsp butter for frying

Cook potatoes in boiling water until tender; drain, reserving water. Place in a large bowl. Beat at medium speed with electric beater until well-mashed. Add milk, salt and pepper and beat until fluffy. In the same saucepan as potatoes were cooked in, cook cabbage in reserved potato water for 6 to 8 minutes until tender. Drain. Meanwhile, melt 2 tbsp butter in a frying pan and sauté onion until tender. Add mashed potato and cooked cabbage to the onion. Heat thoroughly, stirring constantly. Place in a heated serving dish. Serve hot, topped with butter. *Serves 6.*

Princess Potatoes

My friend's German grandmother adapted this recipe to suit Canadian palates. The German dish is called *Prinzesskartoffeln.*

6 medium potatoes, cooked and peeled
2 slices Canadian-style bacon, diced
2 tbsp chopped onion
2 tbsp butter
1 tbsp all-purpose flour
1½ cup milk
salt and pepper to taste

Cook bacon and onion in butter. Stir in flour and slowly add milk. Cook over low heat until sauce is thickened and smooth. Cut cooked potatoes into half-inch squares; add to sauce. Season to taste with salt and pepper. *Serves 6.*

Potato Kugel

A Jewish dish, often served at the Jewish New Year. The potatoes and carrots should be grated by hand or in a food processor. A blender will not give good results. Kugel is best served warm.

5 large potatoes, finely grated
3 medium carrots, finely grated
1 large onion, cut finely
⅓ cup matzoh meal
1 tsp baking powder
3 eggs, separated
¼ tsp Tabasco sauce
¼ cup vegetable oil

Combine vegetables; drain off any liquid. Combine matzoh meal and baking powder and stir into vegetables. Beat egg yolks and Tabasco sauce until light; stir into vegetable mixture. Heat oil and quickly stir into other mixture. Fold in stiffly beaten egg whites. Spoon into a greased shallow 9x9-inch baking dish. Bake at 375°F for 1¼ hours, until golden. Let rest 10 minutes before serving.
Serves 6.

Cheesy Potato Cakes

2 cups mashed potato
2 tbsp minced onion
⅛ tsp pepper
¼ tsp salt
2 tbsp chopped parsley
1 egg, well-beaten
½ cup grated cheddar cheese
¼ cup all-purpose flour or cornmeal

Combine all ingredients. Shape into cakes. Roll in flour or cornmeal. Fry in small amounts of hot fat until golden brown.
Makes 6 patties.

Frozen French fries are the top-selling frozen food item in most supermarkets in North America.

Lefse

Lefse is served buttered and topped with jam or honey. A national Norwegian dish that makes a delicious breakfast treat.

2 cups mashed potato (use baking potatoes as they are drier)
2 tbsp butter
¼ cup cream
½ tsp granulated sugar
1 tsp salt
1 cup all-purpose flour
oil for frying

Combine potato, butter, cream, sugar and salt. Beat until smooth. Cover and refrigerate until cold. Gradually add flour, working in well by kneading with your hands. Divide the dough into small balls and roll very thinly. Fry in oil in a hot skillet or electric frying pan until browned, turn and brown other side. Put lefse on a large plate and cover with a damp towel while remaining cakes are being cooked. To serve, butter each flat cake, roll loosely and slice in diagonal slices. Sprinkle with extra sugar and top with jam or honey.
Yields about 15 (6") cakes.

Crusty Potato Logs

From the kitchen of Brenda Rogers, Linkletter Road, P.E.I.

6 medium potatoes, mashed
¼ cup soft butter
1 tsp salt
¼ tsp thyme
⅛ tsp pepper
3 egg yolks
1 egg, beaten
1½ cups crushed corn flakes

Preheat oven to 425°F. Combine potato, butter, salt, thyme, pepper and egg yolks. Beat with an electric mixer until creamy. Shape into logs (about 2 tbsp of mixture for each). Dip in beaten egg and roll in crushed corn flakes. Place on a greased baking sheet. Bake 15 to 20 minutes. Serve hot.
Note: These can be made early in the day, refrigerated and heated when ready to serve.
Makes 12 logs; serves 6.

Company Croquettes

A nice way to serve potatoes for a company dinner. Deep-fried and crispy.

2 eggs
2 cups warm mashed potato
½ tsp salt
few grains pepper
2 tbsp butter
¼ tsp celery salt
1 tbsp water
¼ cup all-purpose flour
1 cup bread crumbs
fat for deep frying (375°F)

Beat one egg. Combine beaten egg, potato and seasonings. Heat in a saucepan, stirring constantly until mixture leaves the sides of the pan. Cool. Mold into small balls. Beat other egg with water. Roll croquettes in flour, dip in egg and roll in bread crumbs. Deep fry until well-browned. Serve hot.
Makes 12 croquettes.

Barbecue-Herbed Potato Wedges

This recipe from the kitchen of Brenda Rogers makes the nicest herbed potatoes I have eaten. Excellent with barbecued meats or poultry.

2 tbsp margarine
¼ cup olive oil
¼ cup chopped onion
3 tbsp fresh chopped parsley
1 tsp chili powder
¼ tsp garlic powder
¼ tsp basil
¼ tsp salt
dash of pepper
6 medium potatoes

Melt margarine and combine with olive oil. Butter a large piece of heavy aluminum foil. Combine chopped onion, herbs and seasonings. Scrub potatoes and cut in half-inch thick wedges, cutting the potatoes lengthwise. Place potatoes on foil. Brush with margarine and oil mixture. Sprinkle with herbs. Seal the edges of foil. Place on grill about 4 inches from coals and cook until tender for 30 to 45 minutes.
Serves 6.

Potato Applesauce Bake

Don't let this applesauce surprise you! Many countries combine apples with potatoes. This recipe is delicious with pork chops or fried chicken.

4 cups mashed potato
3 tbsp butter
3 tbsp milk
½ tsp salt
⅛ tsp pepper
2 cups applesauce
¼ tsp cinnamon
¼ cup diced onion
1 tbsp parsley
1 tbsp butter
paprika

Preheat oven to 350°F. In a large bowl combine mashed potato with butter, milk, salt and pepper. Beat well. Put a layer of this mixture in the bottom of a well-greased 1½-quart casserole. Mix cinnamon and applesauce. Spread half this mixture over the potatoes. Sprinkle with chopped onion, celery salt and parsley. Drip butter over mixture. Repeat layers and end with a layer of potatoes on top. Sprinkle with paprika. Bake 25 to 30 minutes until heated through.
Serves 4 to 6.

Main-Dish Meals

All meal-planning centres around the main dish. Potatoes have been chosen by great cooks from around the world to combine with ingredients such as meat, fish, poultry and cheese in a variety of main-dish meals.

Choose from a collection of fun-to-make, easy-to-serve dishes. The recipes included have many make-ahead meals as well as last-minute, quick-and-easy dishes.

For most of the world, meat and fish are expensive, luxury items. People of North America are fortunate to eat meat or fish nearly every day. However, when any product is readily available, there can be a tendency to waste. Recipes here are geared to prevent waste and save money while providing good nutrition.

(Note: in these recipes, peeling potatoes is optional unless specifically stated.)

Meat-and-Potato Loaf

Serve with cooked vegetables or a green salad.

2 pounds ground beef
2 cups finely shredded potatoes
1 cup crushed soda crackers
1 large onion, chopped
½ cup chopped green pepper

199

2 eggs
1 cup beef broth (may be made with bouillon cube)
1 tsp marjoram
½ tsp basil
¼ tsp thyme
1 tsp salt
¼ tsp pepper

Combine all ingredients. Pour into a 9x5-inch loaf pan. Bake at 375°F for approximately 1 hour.

Optional Glaze
3 tbsp brown sugar
4 tbsp ketchup
¼ tsp nutmeg
1 tsp dry mustard

Mix together and spread over meat-and-potato mixture before baking. *Serves 6 to 8.*

Potatoburger Pie

A hearty meal-in-a-dish that comes from England. I like to serve this pie with hot potato biscuits.

1 medium onion, chopped
1 tbsp vegetable oil
1 pound ground beef
¾ tsp salt
dash of pepper
2 cups drained cooked green beans (or vegetable of your choice)
1 can (10½ oz) condensed tomato soup
2 cups warm seasoned mashed potato
½ cup grated cheddar cheese (optional)

Preheat oven to 350°F. Cook onion in oil until tender but not brown. Add meat and seasonings; brown lightly. Add beans and soup. Pour into a greased 1½-quart casserole dish. Drop mashed potato by spoonfuls on top. If desired, sprinkle with cheese. Bake for 25 to 30 minutes or until browned.
Serves 4 to 6.

Homesteaders' Boiled Dinner

Next time you have a baked ham, save the bone while there's still a bit of meat left on it and make an old-fashioned boiled dinner.

1 ham bone (with about 2 cups of meat left on)
2 large onions, quartered
2 cups turnips, cut in wedges
6 carrots, cut in large chunks
6 medium potatoes, quartered
salt and pepper to taste

Barely cover ham bone with water. Boil until meat falls from the bone. Add onion and turnip, boil 10 minutes; add carrot, boil 10 minutes. Add potatoes and boil until just tender. Season with salt and pepper. (Be careful with salt as there is usually enough in the ham.)

Red Flannel Hash
** If you happen to have any leftover boiled dinner, drain off the cooking juices and combine any leftover vegetables, mashing with a potato masher. Add any bits of chopped ham. Combine this mixture with an equal quantity of mashed cooked beets. Fry in vegetable oil over medium heat until crusty on the bottom, turn and heat through. Serve as a quick lunch, with biscuits and chow-chow.

Mock-Duck Dinner

This recipe goes back a couple of generations. It was given to me by my sister-in-law, Alberta Reeves of Freetown, P.E.I.

1½ lbs ground beef
2 medium onions, diced
2 cups cubed potato
2 cups sliced carrot
1 cup cubed turnip
2 cups sliced parsnip
4 cups Potato Poultry Dressing (see Miscellaneous)

Brown ground beef loosely in a frying pan. Spread in the bottom of a large baking dish. Simmer vegetables in a small amount of water until barely tender. Drain and spread over ground beef. Top with poultry dressing. Bake at 350°F for approximately 30 minutes until thoroughly heated.
Serves 4 to 6.

Mushroom, Pork and Potato Scallop

This casserole may also be cooked in a microwave on medium for 20 minutes, rotating the dish a half-turn after 10 minutes. Let stand 5 minutes before serving if cooked this way.

4 potatoes, peeled and sliced
1 medium onion, sliced
4 pork chops
1 tsp seasoned salt
¼ tsp pepper
1 cup sliced fresh mushrooms
1 can (10 oz) cream of mushroom soup
½ cup milk

Arrange potato and onion slices in a glass baking dish. Place chops on top of vegetables, sprinkle with seasoned salt and pepper and top with mushrooms. Mix soup and milk; stir until smooth and pour over chops and vegetables. Cover. Bake at 350°F for approximately 1 hour.
Serves 2 to 4.

Pierogi Casserole

15 lasagna noodles
2 cups cottage cheese
1 large egg
¼ tsp onion salt
1 cup shredded cheddar cheese
2 cups mashed potato
¼ tsp salt
⅛ tsp pepper
¼ tsp onion salt
1 cup butter or margarine
1 cup chopped onion

Cook noodles as directed on package. Drain. Spread 5 noodles on the bottom of a 13x9-inch baking dish. In a medium-sized bowl combine cottage cheese, egg and onion salt. Spread over noodles. Cover with 5 more noodles. Combine cheddar cheese, potatoes, salt, pepper and onion salt. Spread over noodles. Cover with remaining noodles. Melt butter in frying pan. Sauté onions slowly until clear and limp. Pour over noodles. Cover. Bake 30 minutes in 350°F oven. Let stand 10 minutes before cutting. Serve with sour cream.
Serves 8.

Pierogi

This recipe from Poland yields about twenty pierogi.

Cheese filling
1 cup cottage cheese
1 tsp melted butter or margarine
3 tbsp sugar
½ tsp cinnamon

Dough
2 eggs
½ cup water
2 cups all-purpose flour
½ tsp salt
1 cup cold mashed potato

water for boiling
butter or margarine
breadcrumbs

Filling: Cream cheese with melted butter. Add sugar and cinnamon and mix well.
Dough: Combine all ingredients in a bowl and blend until barely mixed. Divide dough in half and roll thinly on a floured board. Cut into circles with a large cookie cutter. Place a small amount of filling on one side of circle. Moisten the edges of circle with water and fold dough over filling. Press edges firmly together. Seal edges well to keep filling from running out. Press with fork tines. Carefully drop pierogi into boiling salted water, using a slotted spoon. Do not overcrowd. Cook about 12 minutes. Drain. Fry in butter before serving and sprinkle with fine bread crumbs.
Serves 4 to 6.

Cornish Pasties

Pastry
2 cups all-purpose flour
1 cup mashed potato
1 tsp salt
1 tsp sugar
¾ cup shortening

Meat Mixture
1 lb ground beef
2 large potatoes, peeled and diced (¼-inch cubes)
1 cup finely chopped onion
1 tbsp freshly chopped parsley
1 tsp salt
½ tsp pepper
1 tsp Worcestershire sauce
¼ tsp hot pepper sauce

Preheat oven to 375°F. Combine flour, potato, salt, sugar and shortening. Blend with a pastry blender and form into a ball. Divide into two equal pieces and roll on a lightly floured board. Cut into 24 5-inch circles. Combine all other ingredients; mix well. Spoon about 1 tbsp meat mixture on each circle of pastry; fold and crimp edges to seal the pasties. Bake for 45 minutes or until crust is browned. Serve hot or cold. Can also be reheated.
Makes 24 pasties.

In England, potatoes were once thought to "increase seed and provoke lust."

Duchess Sautéed Beef Liver

This recipe from France turns liver and onions into a celebration.

2 egg yolks
4 cups mashed potato, seasoned with salt and pepper
¼ cup all-purpose flour
1½ tsp salt
¼ tsp pepper
1½ lbs sliced beef liver
2 tbsp vegetable oil
2 medium onions, sliced
1 green pepper, seeded and cut in wedges
1 tomato, cut in thin slices
1½ cups water
1 tbsp beef bouillon base

Preheat oven to 400°F. Beat egg yolk into mashed potato. Pipe potato in a border around the edge of a large casserole or baking dish. (If you do not have a pastry bag, use an ice-cream scoop to make small mounds around the dish.) Bake for 15 minutes, until heated through. Meanwhile, combine flour, salt and pepper on waxed paper. Cut liver in serving-sized pieces and coat with flour. Sauté liver in hot oil in a large skillet for 4 minutes on each side. In casserole arrange slices in an overlapping fashion inside the border of potatoes. Turn oven temperature to lowest possible setting and keep liver and potato mixture warm. Sauté onion and green peppers in the same skillet, adding more oil if necessary, for about 10 minutes. Slice tomatoes and add to the skillet. Sauté 2 minutes longer. Arrange vegetables on top of liver. Add water and soup base to skillet. Bring to a boil, stirring and scraping the pan to dissolve any brown bits. Simmer uncovered. Pour over liver. Serve at once.
Serves 4 to 6.

Some Bhutanese blamed the potato for stomach problems. It was found later that they were eaten with large helpings of hot chili peppers.

Spicy Beef and Potato Hot Pot

Make four generous servings with only one pound of steak. Serve with
cheese biscuits, hot from the oven.

1 lb boneless steak, cut in small cubes
2 tbsp all-purpose flour
2 tbsp vegetable oil
1 medium onion, chopped
½ cup chopped celery
1 clove garlic, minced
4 to 5 medium potatoes, peeled and cubed
1 can (8 oz) tomato sauce
½ cup water
2 tbsp cider vinegar
1 tbsp Worcestershire sauce
2 tsp dry mustard
¼ tsp Tabasco sauce
dash ground red pepper
salt and pepper to taste

Preheat oven to 350°F. Coat meat with flour. Heat oil in a large skillet
over medium heat. Cook meat until browned. Add onion, celery and
garlic. Cook until limp. Add remaining ingredients. Cook until meat
and potatoes are well-coated with spices and oil. Place in a 2-quart
casserole dish. Cover and bake for 1½ hours until meat and potatoes
are tender.
Serves 4.

Note: Some potatoes take longer to cook than others. I find Russet
Burbanks take nearly 2 hours to cook in this casserole.

Pot Roast Supreme

1 3-lb boneless rump roast
1 tbsp vegetable oil
2 cups beef bouillon
1 tbsp horse radish
1 bay leaf
1 clove garlic, minced
3 medium carrots, cut in 2-inch pieces
6 medium potatoes, peeled and quartered
1 small turnip, peeled and cut in large cubes
1 medium cabbage (about 2 lbs) cut in 6 wedges
½ cup water
1 tbsp cornstarch

In a large saucepan or Dutch oven brown meat in oil. Pour off any excess fat and discard. Add bouillon, horse radish, bay leaf and garlic; cover and cook over low heat. After about 2 hours, add carrot, potatoes and turnip. Cook 30 minutes, stirring occasionally. Set cabbage on top of other ingredients (without stirring) and cook 30 minutes longer. Remove bay leaf before serving. Remove meat and vegetables and place on a serving platter; keep warm. Meanwhile, blend water with cornstarch until smooth. Slowly stir into cooking liquid. Cook, stirring until thickened. Pour over meat and vegetables on platter. Serve at once. *Serves 6 to 8.*

Potato Patchwork Casserole

This casserole freezes well. I like to double the recipe and freeze half.

1 lb ground beef
1 medium green pepper, chopped
½ cup chopped onion
4 cups cubed cooked potatoes
1 can (8 oz) tomato sauce
1 can (3 oz) tomato paste
½ cup water
½ tsp salt
dash pepper
¼ tsp basil
2 cups thinly sliced cheddar cheese

Preheat oven to 350°F. Brown meat loosely in a frying pan. Add green pepper and onion and cook until tender. Stir in potatoes, tomato sauce, tomato paste, water, salt, pepper and basil. Spoon half of this mixture into a baking dish. Cover with half the cheese slices. Top with remaining potato mixture. Cover dish and bake in preheated oven for 45 minutes. Uncover. Top with remaining cheese slices, cut in decorative shapes and arrange in a patchwork design. Let stand 5 minutes or until cheese melts. Serve hot.
Serves 6.

Christmas Tourtière

A prize-winning recipe that makes a delicious Christmas Eve buffet dish, served with cranberry sauce and tossed salad.

pastry for 2 double-crust pies
1½ lbs minced pork
1 clove garlic, minced
1 medium cooking onion, diced
½ tsp thyme
½ tsp sage
¼ tsp ginger
½ tsp dry mustard
⅛ tsp cloves
1½ tsp salt
½ tsp allspice
2 medium potatoes, mashed
½ cup potato water

Combine pork, garlic, onion and seasonings in a frying pan. Cook until meat is tender. Add mashed potato and stir. Cool. Preheat oven to 400°F. Line 2 pie plates with pastry. Pour filling into pie plates; cover with remaining pastry. Slash top to allow steam to escape. Bake until crust is brown.
* Note: These pies freeze well after baking, or can be prepared, frozen (unbaked) and baked when needed.
Each pie serves 6.

Hollywood used flaked potatoes to simulate snow in their early movies.

Olde English Meat Pie

A meat pie with a difference—this tasty recipe uses beef liver.

1 lb beef liver
¼ cup all-purpose flour
1 tsp salt
¼ tsp pepper
¼ cup vegetable oil
2½ cups sliced carrot
4 to 5 medium potatoes, sliced
1½ cups sliced onion
2 tsp instant beef broth
½ tsp sage or thyme

Cut beef liver into 1½-inch squares; coat with a mixture of flour, salt and pepper. Brown liver a bit at a time in hot oil in a large skillet. Remove with a slotted spoon to an 8-cup casserole dish. Pare and slice carrot and potatoes; cook in salt water (barely to top of vegetables) for 10 minutes. Remove with a slotted spoon to casserole, reserving liquid. Sauté onions in drippings in skillet until soft. Add water to vegetable cooking liquid to make 2 cups; stir into skillet with beef broth and sage or thyme. Pour over vegetables and liver in casserole. Bake at 400°F for about 40 minutes.
Serves 6.

Scottish Shepherd's Pie

A traditional dish from Scotland, this pie is easy to prepare and always welcome.

½ lb chopped cooked beef
1 small onion, cooked and chopped
1 tsp ketchup
salt and pepper to taste
1 cup leftover gravy
2 cups seasoned mashed potato
2 tbsp butter or margarine
cayenne pepper
parsley flakes

Preheat oven to 350°F. Mix together meat, onion, ketchup, salt, pepper and gravy. Place in a greased baking dish. Cover with mashed potato. Dot with small pieces of butter. Bake for 20 to 30 minutes. Sprinkle with cayenne pepper and decorate with a little parsley. Serve hot. *Serves 2.*

Variation: This pie can be made using any type of meat and gravy, or by substituting cooked white fish and a tasty white sauce or creamed soup for the meat and gravy.

Old-Fashioned Turkey Vegetable Pie

An excellent way to serve that leftover Christmas turkey.

pastry or biscuit dough to cover a 2½-quart casserole
3 cups cubed leftover cooked turkey
3 cups cubed cooked potatoes
1 cup diced carrot
½ cup chopped onion
½ cup chopped celery
½ cup finely cubed turnip
½ tsp salt
¼ tsp pepper
¼ tsp oregano
1 cup water
⅔ cup thawed frozen peas
2 cups leftover turkey gravy **or**
    1 can (10 oz) cream of celery soup

Preheat oven to 350°F. Place turkey, potato, carrot, onion, celery and turnip in a casserole dish. Sprinkle with seasonings. Add water and stir. Cover and bake at 350°F for one hour. Add peas and bake another 15 minutes. Drain liquid from casserole and combine with gravy or soup. Pour over casserole. Cover with pie crust or biscuit topping. Slash top to let steam escape. Bake at 425°F for 20 minutes or until golden brown.
Serves 6.

Almost any part of a potato can produce more potatoes; seed pieces, true potato seed or cuttings from the plant.

Râpure

A popular Acadian recipe.

18 large potatoes
1 cup hot mashed potato
2 cups bread crumbs
1½ tsp salt
pepper to taste
2 medium onions, chopped finely
½ cup rendered pork fat
4 to 5 lb stewing chicken, cooked and cut in small pieces
⅓ cup milk
2 eggs
2 tbsp baking powder

Peel potatoes and grate very finely. Drain liquid. Preheat oven to 350°F.
Add mashed potato, bread crumbs, salt and pepper to grated potatoes.
Sauté onion in a small amount of pork fat. Combine chicken and onion
with potato mixture. Beat milk, eggs and baking powder and mix with
other ingredients. Put remaining pork fat in a large pan (12x16-inch)
and heat. Mix about half the fat into potato mixture. Pour mixture into
hot pan; pour over remaining fat. Bake for 2 hours or until brown and
crusty. Cut in squares and serve with molasses.
Serves 10 to 12.

Variation: Cubed cooked pork may be used in place of chicken, or recipe
can be made without meat.

Hungarian Goulash

One cup of light cream may be substituted for the canned tomatoes in
this recipe.

2 pounds beef, cut in 1-inch cubes
2 medium onions, thinly sliced
½ cup margarine or butter
1 tsp salt
¼ tsp pepper
½ tsp paprika
1 cup canned tomatoes
4 medium potatoes, diced

Sauté meat and onions in margarine until browned. Add seasonings and tomatoes. Simmer for 30 minutes. Add potatoes and simmer an additional 30 minutes.
Serves 6.

Note: If goulash seems too dry, add ¼ to ½ cup water

Chicken-Potato Stir-Fry

Fries go Oriental when stirred up with chicken and snow peas. This recipe comes from the Potato Board of Denver, Colorado.

6 to 8 ounces skinned and boned chicken breasts
4 tsp cornstarch
1 clove garlic, halved
2 tbsp vegetable oil
1½ cups frozen French fries
1½ cups trimmed snow peas
1 cup sliced mushrooms
⅓ cup teriyaki sauce
⅓ cup water
1 medium tomato, cut into wedges

Pound chicken breasts with a rolling pin to flatten slightly. Cut into ¼-inch strips. Toss with cornstarch to coat; set aside. In a large wok or skillet, over high heat cook garlic in 1 tbsp oil until lightly browned. Discard garlic. Add frozen French fries to wok; stir-fry about 5 minutes until lightly browned and cooked through. Remove with a slotted spoon to paper towelling. Heat the remaining oil in wok. Add chicken. Stir-fry over high heat for 2 minutes. Add snow peas and mushrooms. Stir-fry about 3 minutes, until chicken is opaque and snow peas are tender-crisp. Stir in teriyaki sauce and water. Add tomato and reserved potatoes. Toss gently, just until heated through. Serve immediately.
Serves 2.

In Indonesia, potatoes are reserved for special occasions, such as wed-dings and birthdays.

Chicken Fricot (with Dumplings)

An ever-popular Acadian dish dating back to the early pioneers. This recipe comes from Rita Arsenault of Abram's Village, P.E.I.

1 broiler chicken, cut in serving-sized pieces
¼ cup butter or margarine
1 medium onion, chopped
6 cups water
4 to 5 cups peeled and cubed potatoes
1 tbsp salt
pepper to taste

In a large saucepan, fry chicken slowly in butter for about 30 minutes. Add chopped onion and fry another 10 to 15 minutes. Cover with boiling water. Cover pot and simmer until chicken is lightly tender. Add potatoes, salt and pepper and continue cooking while preparing dumplings.

Dumplings
1 cup all-purpose flour
¼ tsp salt
1½ tsp baking powder
cold water

Combine flour, salt, baking powder and enough water to make a soft, slightly sticky dough. Drop dumplings by teaspoon into fricot. Cover and cook an additional 15 minutes. Do not remove cover while dumplings are cooking. Serve hot.
Serves 6 to 8.

Meredith's Mashie Burgers

"Leftover mashed potatoes are prized in the Potato Museum kitchen," according to Meredith Hughes. "They form a thickener for soups, add moisture and minerals to muffins, and mixed with chopped vegetables and fried will feed the hungry hordes as Meredith's Mashie Burgers."

2 cups leftover mashed potato
1 egg, lightly beaten
2 tbsp whole wheat flour
½ cup chopped scallions
2 tbsp fresh chopped parsley
¾ cup grated cheddar cheese
½ cup chopped walnuts
½ cup chopped mushrooms
1 large carrot, grated
freshly ground black pepper
salt to taste
heaping tbsp chopped fresh dill (optional)
olive oil for frying

Combine all ingredients in a large bowl, mixing them as you would a meat-loaf preparation. Form into patties and fry on both sides in olive oil until lightly browned. Serve on hamburger rolls or toasted bread. *Makes 6 burgers.*

House Bankin'

An easily prepared pioneer recipe that is sure to please.

1 lb salt cod
4 medium raw potatoes, sliced
6 slices bacon
1 large onion, sliced

Soak cod for 3 hours in cold water. Cut into small pieces. Drain, cover with cold water and simmer over low heat for 15 minutes. Add peeled, sliced potatoes and cook until potatoes are tender. Meanwhile, cut bacon into small pieces and fry until crisp. Remove from pan and set aside. Sauté onion rings in pan drippings until soft and clear. Drain fish and potatoes. Place in a serving bowl. Pour bacon, onion and drippings over the fish. Serve immediately while very hot with bannock and molasses. *Serves 4 to 6.*

All-Purpose Hash

Almost any meat or fish will make a delicious hash. A super way to use leftover roast beef, poultry, pork, ham, corned beef or fish.

1 cup chopped onion
1 clove garlic, crushed (optional)
¼ cup butter or margarine
2 tbsp bacon drippings or vegetable oil
4 medium potatoes, cooked and cubed
½ tsp salt
¼ tsp pepper
¼ tsp thyme
3 cups cubed cooked meat
2 tbsp water

Sauté onion and garlic in butter and bacon drippings until tender. Add potatoes, salt, pepper and thyme. Cook over medium heat until potatoes are golden. Add meat and water. Heat thoroughly.
Serves 6.

Variation: Form hash into small mounds (about the size of a hamburger pattie). Hollow slightly in centre. Add an egg to each mound. Cover and simmer 3 to 4 minutes, until eggs are set.

White Fish Soufflé

Almost any white fish can be used for this dish. Easy and economical.

1 lb cold cooked fish, flaked
2 tbsp grated carrot
2 tbsp grated onion
½ tsp salt
½ tsp pepper
4 eggs, separated
2 cups mashed potato (seasoned to taste with salt and pepper)
2 tbsp melted butter or margarine

Preheat oven to 350°F. Combine fish, carrot, onion, salt and pepper. Beat egg yolks and add to this mixture. Stir in mashed potato and melted butter. Fold in stiffly beaten egg whites. Spread in a greased baking dish. Set in a pan of warm water in the centre of the oven. Bake 30 minutes.
Serves 4 to 6.

Quick Fish Cakes

Canned chicken haddie makes these fish cakes quick to make.

2 medium onions, chopped
⅓ cup water
2 cups chicken haddie, drained and flaked
8 medium potatoes, cooked and mashed
4 parsnips, cooked and mashed
½ tsp salt (or to taste)
¼ tsp pepper
1 egg, well-beaten
½ cup fine bread crumbs
fat for frying (such as bacon drippings)

Cook onions in water. Do not drain. Add fish and vegetables; season with salt and pepper. Add egg and mix well. Form into patties. Roll in bread crumbs. Fry in bacon drippings or other fat.
Makes 12 to 16 patties.

Sea Cakes

A recipe from the P.E.I. Department of Fisheries.

1 can (15 oz) mackerel
¼ cup chopped onion
1 egg, beaten
2 cups mashed potato
1 tsp salt
½ tsp pepper
1 tbsp ketchup
1 cup dry bread crumbs
½ cup melted butter or margarine

Preheat oven to 450°F. Rinse, drain, skin and flake mackerel. Combine fish, onion, egg, potatoes, salt, pepper and ketchup. Mix well. Shape into 12 cakes and roll in bread crumbs. Place on a well-greased baking pan. Brush with melted margarine. Bake for 8 minutes, or until browned on bottom. Turn carefully and bake 3 to 5 minutes longer or until brown on both sides.
Serves 6.

Buffet Seafood Elegante

⅓ cup butter or margarine
1 small onion, chopped
2 tbsp all-purpose flour
1½ cups milk
3 raw potatoes, peeled and sliced
½ lb white fish fillets, cut in pieces
1 small can (7 oz) shrimp, drained
1 tsp dry parsley
1 can (10 oz) sliced mushrooms, drained

Cook onion in melted butter over medium heat until transparent. Gradually stir in flour, blending well. Cook 1 minute, stirring constantly. Slowly add milk and cook until mixture is smooth and thick, stirring constantly. Line a buttered casserole with potato slices. Arrange fish and shrimp over potatoes. Sprinkle with parsley and mushrooms. Pour sauce over the casserole and place in oven. Cook 40 minutes at 375°F until potatoes are tender.
Serves 4 to 6.

Tuna Puff Casserole

A light and delicious casserole, combining two old favourites, potatoes and tuna.

2 cans (7 oz) tuna, drained and flaked
2 tbsp finely minced onion
2 tbsp chopped fresh parsley
dash pepper
1 cup cooked peas
4 cups mashed potato
2 egg yolks
2 egg whites
2 tbsp melted butter or margarine
½ tsp salt

Combine tuna, onion, parsley, pepper, peas, potatoes and egg yolks. Mix well. Beat egg whites until soft peaks form; add to potato and fish mixture. Mix in melted butter and salt. Put in a greased casserole and bake at 450°F for 20 minutes until nicely browned.
Serves 4.

Variation: Salmon may be used instead of tuna.

Clam Casserole

½ cup melted butter or margarine
2 tbsp all-purpose flour
1 cup evaporated milk
2 small cans (10 oz) baby clams and juice
1 cup finely chopped onion
3 cups diced raw potato
1 tsp salt
¼ tsp pepper
1 tsp celery seed
2 tbsp parsley flakes
4 hard-cooked eggs, quartered
1 cup soft bread crumbs

Melt butter and put in the bottom of a casserole dish. Add flour and mix until blended. Stir in milk and clam juice; mix well to dissolve any lumps. Add clams, onion, potato and seasonings. Mix into sauce. Gently mix in hard-cooked eggs so as not to break them up. Sprinkle with breadcrumbs. Bake covered for 20 minutes at 350°F. Remove cover and bake until potato is cooked and casserole is lightly browned on top. *Serves 6.*

Before the convenience of electric heating and cooking stoves, Grandma used to throw raw potato peelings in her wood stove and fireplace to remove soot and creosote build-up. I don't know why this works, but I've tried it and it does.

Fish and Potato Scallop

P.E.I.'s most popular foods combine for a new twist to an old favourite.

1 lb white fish (cod, haddock, sole, for example)
2 tbsp lemon juice
¼ cup butter or margarine, divided
2 tbsp all-purpose flour
2 cups milk
1½ tsp finely minced onion
1 tsp salt
¼ tsp pepper
2 cups peas and carrots (partially cooked)
4 cups diced potato (partially cooked)
⅛ tsp nutmeg
¾ cup cracker crumbs

Partially cook potatoes in a small amount of water. Drain. Cut fish into 1-inch cubes. Cover with boiling water and lemon juice. Heat 2 tbsp margarine. Add flour and stir until bubbling. Stir in onion and milk. Cook until thick in a double boiler. Season with salt and pepper. Fold in partially cooked vegetables and nutmeg. Drain fish. Mix fish with the vegetable mixture. Place in a casserole. Melt remaining butter; add to cracker crumbs. Sprinkle over casserole. Bake at 350°F for 30 to 45 minutes or until vegetables are cooked through.
Serves 6.

Potatoes are hailed as a cure for gout, lumbago, black eyes, sunburn, rheumatism, sore throats, toothaches, temper tantrums and drunkenness.
Potatoes have been said to cause rickets, indigestion, syphilis, leprosy, lust and warts.

Miscellaneous

This section will show the diverse qualities of the potato. Here, in a collection of recipes that includes pancake syrup, mayonnaise, hot chocolate, pizza, pastry and pudding sauce to name a few, we find the ever-capable potato.

Potato Water

Because I usually save potato water in a container in my refrigerator, I don't generally have to "make" potato water. But just in case, here is the way to get the most nutrients from your potatoes.

2 medium potatoes
2½ cups water

Boil potatoes with peelings on. Be careful not to cook too long; if potatoes break up, water will be cloudy. Do not cut potatoes before cooking. Water should look much like apple juice.

Potato Pastry

1½ cups all-purpose flour
½ tsp salt
½ cup lard or shortening
¼ cup mashed potato
1 egg yolk

Preheat oven to 350°F. Combine flour and salt and cut in lard until mixture is crumbly. Add mashed potato and egg yolk. Toss with a fork until a ball is formed. (Do not add water.) Divide into two balls. Roll with a light even pressure to form a circle an inch larger than the inverted pie plate. Place pastry in pie plate. Prick with a fork and bake 12 to 15 minutes.
Makes 2 9-inch pie shells or 1 double-crust pie.

Never-Fail Potato Pastry

This light and buttery "Never-Fail" pastry is from Australia.

2½ cups all-purpose flour
½ tsp salt
1 tsp baking powder
1 cup butter or margarine
⅔ cup mashed potato

Sift together flour, salt and baking powder. Add butter and blend with a pastry blender until mixture resembles fine crumbs. Add potato and blend with the pastry blender or fork until well-mixed. Place in refrigerator for at least 1 hour before using. Preheat oven to 450°F. Roll on a floured board. Fit into a pie plate and prick with a fork. Bake for 10 minutes. Fill with desired filling.
Makes 2 9-inch pie shells.

Jack Simplot of Idaho is said to have the world's largest potato farm: 30,000 acres. He is called "the Potato King" and "Mr. Spud."

Potato Maple Syrup

Try this delicious, economical syrup on ice cream, pancakes or in recipes such as Potato Syrup Pie. Keeps well in refrigerator.

2 cups clear potato water*
2 cups granulated sugar
few shakes salt
1 tsp maple flavouring

Combine potato water, sugar and salt. Bring to a full rolling boil and boil rapidly for 10 minutes. Add maple flavouring. Cool. Store in a glass bottle in refrigerator for up to four months.
Makes 2 cups.

Potato Mayonnaise

Serve with cold meat. Keep refrigerated.

1 cup mashed potato
4 tbsp olive oil or salad oil
6 tbsp vinegar
2 tsp horse radish
1 tsp Worcestershire sauce
½ tsp salt
½ tsp dry mustard
½ tsp granulated sugar

Combine all ingredients and mix well. Keeps for up to two weeks in refrigerator.
Makes 1½ cups.

Potato Submarines

A good choice for hearty teenage appetites, and it's highly nutritious.

2 cups cooked and diced potatoes
½ cup mayonnaise
1 tsp prepared mustard
¼ cup chopped onion
⅓ cup shredded cheese
¾ cup chopped celery
1 can sardines, drained and chopped
2 hard-cooked eggs, chopped
1 tsp salt
¼ tsp pepper
3 small-sized submarine buns
1 dill pickle, seeded and sliced into 6 equal pieces for garnish

Add mayonnaise and mustard to potatoes and let stand 15 minutes. Combine onion, cheese, celery, sardines, eggs, salt and pepper. Mix potatoes with other ingredients. Halve submarine rolls down the centre lengthwise. Spoon in the potato mixture. Garnish with dill pickle.
Serves 6.

Potato-Water Pudding Sauce

There is no end to the ways you can use this easy pudding sauce recipe. Try it on Cottage Pudding, Carrot and Potato Pudding or Blueberry Cake, to name a few.

1 cup brown sugar
⅛ tsp salt
2 tbsp cornstarch
2 cups potato water
1½ tsp vanilla
1 tsp lemon juice
1 tbsp butter or margarine

Mix brown sugar, salt and cornstarch. Add potato water. Bring to a boil. Simmer until thick and clear. Add vanilla, lemon juice and butter; stir. Serve hot.
Makes 2 cups.

Potato Pizza

This recipe comes from Australia. A quick-to-make pizza that is chock full of flavour.

Crust
1 cup cooked sieved potato
2 tbsp melted butter or margarine
2 tbsp milk
½ tsp salt
1 cup all-purpose flour
½ tsp baking powder

Topping
1 medium onion, finely chopped
½ cup sliced mushrooms
2 tbsp butter or margarine
1 large tomato, thinly sliced
1 cup grated parmesan cheese

Prepare crust by beating together potato, butter, milk and salt. Add flour and baking powder to make a stiff dough. Sauté onion and mushrooms in butter. Cut dough into 5 4-inch circles and cook on a griddle or greased skillet until browned lightly. Transfer to a baking sheet. Place grated cheese and sliced tomatoes on crust. Cover with sautéed onions and mushrooms and sprinkle with parmesan cheese. Brown under a hot broiler.
Makes 5 mini-pizzas.

Turkey Stuffing

A delicious full-flavoured stuffing that can be baked in a casserole or used to stuff a 12 to 15 pound turkey.

1 large onion, minced
½ cup butter or margarine
6 cups mashed potato
6 cups dry bread crumbs
¼ cup chicken soup base powder
½ tsp pepper
1 tbsp poultry seasoning
(This recipe requires no extra salt other than that contained in the soup base.)

Preheat oven to 350°F. Sauté onion in butter over low heat until barely tender. Do not brown. Mix well with remaining ingredients. Place in a greased casserole and bake for 30 minutes or use to stuff the cavity in a turkey and cook in the usual manner.

Note: Save bread as it begins to dry out. I use bread that is about 3 days old. Chop in a blender and store in a glass jar. Bread crumbs that are dried properly will keep several weeks.

Potato Poultry Dressing

This recipe makes enough dressing for one large chicken or small turkey.

⅓ cup butter or margarine
1½ cups chopped onion
1½ cups chopped celery
1½ tsp salt
⅛ tsp pepper
½ tsp poultry seasoning
½ tsp sage
6 cups bread cubes
¼ cup water
1 egg, beaten
2 cups mashed potato

Melt butter; sauté onion and celery. Combine with remaining ingredients. Toss lightly. Use to stuff a large chicken or small turkey.
Serves 6.

Chocolate Syrup

Great on ice cream or to add to hot or cold milk. This syrup will keep for weeks in the refrigerator.

½ cup cocoa
1½ cups granulated sugar
1½ cups boiling potato water
1½ tsp cornstarch
small amount of cold water
1½ tsp vanilla

Mix cocoa and sugar; sift if lumpy. Add boiling potato water. Boil rapidly for 3 minutes. Mix cornstarch with cold water. Add to chocolate mixture. Simmer 5 minutes. Add vanilla. Cool.
Makes 2 cups.

Mock Almond Paste

This recipe was given to me by a professional cake decorator from Vancouver, British Columbia. She uses it regularly in her shop. Lovely for wedding and Christmas cakes.

½ cup mashed potato
½ cup margarine or butter
2 lbs icing sugar
almond flavouring to taste (about 1 tsp)

Beat potato in a mixer until smooth. Add margarine and gradually mix in flavouring and sugar. When too stiff to beat, put on a counter and knead in the rest of the sugar.

In a good year, the Russians are credited with approximately one-third of the world's potato production. Potatoes are called "the second bread of Russia."

Potato Noodles

Next time you serve Stroganoff, try these delicious buttery noodles. This recipe was adapted from a popular Hungarian dish.

5 medium potatoes
1½ tsp salt
2 eggs
1 cup all-purpose flour
4 to 6 tbsp butter or margarine

Boil whole unpeeled potatoes in a small amount of water. Drain. Peel and rice or mash. Add salt, eggs and flour to hot potatoes. Knead on a lightly floured board until dough is easy to roll. Add extra flour if necessary. Preheat oven to 375°F. Roll dough as thinly as possible. Cut into strips about ¼-inch by 4 inches. Let dry for about 20 minutes. Layer noodles in a criss-crossed fashion in a buttered baking dish. Dot with remaining butter. Bake uncovered until nicely browned, 25 to 30 minutes.
Serves 5 to 6.

Potato Chip Crunchy Sandwich

This recipe comes from the kitchen of Cindy Chase of Halifax, Nova Scotia. A healthy snack for young and old alike.

4 strips bacon, cut in half
8 slices cracked or whole wheat bread
soft butter or margarine
peanut butter
1 small bag of potato chips

Sauté bacon until nicely browned. Drain on absorbent paper. Butter 4 slices of bread. Spread peanut butter on remaining bread. Arrange a triple layer of potato chips over peanut butter (good way to use up broken chips). Put two pieces of bacon on each sandwich. Cover with buttered bread. Garnish with pickle or radish roses.
Serves 2.

Ingredient Substitutions

1 tsp *baking powder* (double acting) = 1½ tsp regular baking powder

1 tsp *baking powder* = ¼ tsp baking soda plus ½ tsp cream of tartar

1 cup *butter* = 1 cup margarine

    or ⅞ cup shortening plus ¼ tsp salt

    or ⅞ cup lard plus ¼ tsp salt

1 oz unsweetened *chocolate* = 3 level tbsp cocoa plus 1 tbsp butter, margarine or shortening

1 tbsp *cornstarch* (for thickening) = 2 tbsp flour or 4 tbsp tapioca

1 cup *corn syrup* = 1 cup honey or molasses or 1 cup sugar plus ¼ cup liquid

    (Note: Do not substitute corn syrup when making candies)

¾ cup *cracker crumbs* = 1 cup bread crumbs

Cream: 1 cup *coffee cream* = ⅞ cup milk plus 3 tbsp butter

    1 cup *heavy cream* = ¾ cup milk plus ⅓ cup butter

    1 cup *sour cream* (heavy) = ⅔ cup sour milk plus ⅓ cup butter

    1 cup *sour cream* (light) = ¾ cup sour milk plus 3 tbsp butter

    1 cup *sweet cream* = ¾ cup milk plus ¼ cup butter

Eggs: Never substitute anything for eggs, however . . .

    1 whole egg = 2 egg yolks (for thickening)

    1 whole egg = 2 egg yolks plus 2 tbsp water (in cookies)

    2 large eggs = 3 small eggs

    1 cup whole eggs = 5 to 6 large eggs

    1 cup egg whites = whites of 8 to 10 large eggs

    1 cup egg yolks = yolks of 12 large eggs

Flour: 1 cup sifted *all-purpose flour* = 1 cup plus 2 tbsp cake or pastry flour

    1 cup *pastry flour* = 1 cup minus 2 tbsp all-purpose flour

    1 cup *flour (for breads)* = ½ cup bran, whole wheat flour or cornmeal   plus ½ cup all-purpose flour

    1 cup *unsifted flour* = 1 cup plus 2 tbsp sifted flour

    1 cup *self-raising flour* = 1 cup sifted all-purpose flour plus 1½ tsp   baking power and ¼ tsp salt

1 clove *garlic* = ⅛ tsp garlic powder

1 tbsp *fresh herbs* (parsley flakes, oregano, etc.) = 1 tsp dried herbs

1 cup liquid *honey* = 1 cup corn syrup

    or 1 cup molasses

    or 1 cup sugar plus ¼ cup liquid (i.e., water, milk—whatever liquid recipe   calls for)

1 cup *ketchup* = 1 cup tomato sauce plus ½ cup sugar and 2 tbsp vinegar

Juice of 1 *lemon* = 3 to 4 tbsp bottled lemon juice

1 cup *meat stock* = 1 bouillon cube plus 1 cup water

    or 1 cup consommé

    or 1 rounded tsp soup base powder in 1 cup water

Milk: 1 cup *skim milk* = 1 cup water plus 4 tbsp powdered milk
    1 cup *sour milk* = 1 cup buttermilk
    or
    1 tbsp vinegar or lemon juice and enough milk to fill 1 cup (let
    stand   several minutes)
    1 cup *sweet milk* = ½ cup evaporated milk plus ½ cup water
    or
    (for baking) 1 cup sour milk plus ½ tsp baking soda
    (decrease baking powder in recipe by 2 tsp)
    or
    1 cup reconstituted dry milk plus 2 tbsp margarine
    **Never substitute anything for sweetened condensed milk
1 tsp dry *mustard* = 1 tbsp prepared mustard
**Never substitute oil for shortening or vice versa (except in frying)
1 small fresh *onion* = 1 tbsp onion flakes or minced instant onion
Juice of 1 *orange* = ⅓ cup reconstituted orange juice
Sugar: 1 cup *granulated sugar* = 1 cup brown sugar, firmly packed
    1 cup *sugar* = ¾ cup honey
    or
    1 cup molasses plus ¼ tsp soda (reduce liquid in recipe by ¼ cup)
4 tbsp *tapioca* (to thicken) = 2 tbsp flour or 1 tbsp cornstarch
1 cup canned *tomatoes* = 1⅓ cups fresh tomatoes, peeled and simmered
    for   10 minutes
1 cup *tomato juice* = ½ cup tomato sauce plus ½ cup water
1 cup *tomato sauce* = ½ cup tomato paste plus ½ cup water
1 tbsp *yeast* = 1 envelope dry yeast or 1 cake yeast
1 cup *yogurt* = 1 cup sour milk

Temperature Chart for Deep-Frying

	Temperature of fat	Time in minutes
Croquettes (previously cooked food)	375°	2 to 4
Doughnuts	375°	2 to 3
Fritters	365°–375°	3 to 5
French fries	370°	7
Vegetable rings	375°–380°	3
Oysters or small fish	375°	2 to 5

Oven Temperature Chart

	Fahrenheit	Celsius
Very slow oven	250°–300°	120°–150°
Slow oven	300°–325°	150°–160°
Moderate oven	325°–375°	160°–190°
Moderately hot oven	375°–400°	190°–200°
Hot oven	400°–450°	200°–230°
Very hot oven	450°–500°	230°–260°

Approximate Baking Times in a Preheated Oven

Note: This is an approximate guide. Follow baking times and temperatures given in individual recipes.

	Temperature	Time
Breads:		
coffee cakes	375°	20 to 25 minutes
cornbread	375°	30 minutes
fruit & nut loaves	350°	1 hour
muffins	375°	30 minutes
popovers	450°	15 minutes, then
	350°	20 minutes
tea biscuits	425°	12 to 15 minutes
yeast loaves	375°	30 minutes
yeast rolls	350°	15 to 20 minutes
Cakes:		
angel food	375°	30 minutes
butter (layer)	350°	25 to 30 minutes
butter (square)	350°	50 to 60 minutes
cake mix	350°	30 to 35 minutes
chiffon	325°	1 hour
cup cakes	350°	20 to 25 minutes
fruit cakes	275°	1½ to 3 hours, depending on size of cake
gingerbread	325°	50 to 60 minutes
jelly roll	325°	15 minutes
pound cake	325°	1 to 1¼ hours
sponge cake	325°	1 hour

Cookies:

Drop cookies	350°	8 to 10 minutes
Macaroons	350°	8 to 10 minutes
Meringues	250°	1 hour
Refrigerator	350°	8 to 10 minutes
Rolled	375°	8 to 10 minutes
Shaped	350°	10 to 12 minutes

Pastry:

Butter tarts	375°	20 minutes
Cream puffs	425°	20 minutes, then
	350°	15 to 20 minutes
Double-crust pie	450°	10 minutes, then
	350°	30 to 40 minutes
Eclairs	425°	30 minutes, then
	325°	15 to 20 minutes
Pie & tart shells	450°	10 to 15 minutes
Turnovers	450°	10 minutes, then
	375°	30 minutes
Meringue (on cooked filling)	350°	12 minutes

Table of Imperial Weights and Measures

dash or pinch = less than ⅛ tsp
¼ tsp = 1 saltspoon
1 tsp = 1 coffee spoon
2 tsp = 1 dessert spoon
3 tsp = 1 tbsp
2 tbsp = ⅛ cup or 1 ounce
4 tbsp = ¼ cup
5⅓ tbsp = ⅓ cup
8 tbsp = ½ cup or 1 tea cup
16 tbsp = 1 cup
1 fluid ounce = 2 tbsp
1 pint = 2 cups
1 quart = 2 pints
1 quart = 4 cups
1 gallon = 4 quarts
1 pound = 16 ounces

Approximate Metric Conversions

Imperial Measurements	Approximate Metric Conversion
⅛ tsp	0.5 mL
¼ tsp	1 mL
½ tsp	2 mL
1 tsp	5 mL
1 tbsp	15 mL
1 coffee measure	25 mL
2 tbsp (1 oz)	30 mL
¼ cup	50 mL
⅓ cup	80 mL
½ cup	125 mL
⅔ cup	160 mL
¾ cup	180 mL
1 cup	250 mL
1 pint	625 mL
1 quart	1000 mL or 1.25 litre
¼ pound	125 g
½ pound	250 g
¾ pound	350 g
1 pound	500 g

Converting to Metric

To change	to	Multiply by
teaspoons	mL	5
tablespoons	mL	15
ounces	mL	28
cups	litres	0.24

Casserole sizes

1 quart casserole equals a 1.5 litre casserole
1½ quart casserole equals a 2 litre casserole

Cake pans:

8-inch square	2 litre
9-inch square	2.5 litre
12x8x2-inch	3 litre
13x9x2-inch	3.5 litre
8-inch round	1.2 litre
9-inch round	1.5 litre
jelly roll pan (15x10-inch)	2 litre

Pie pans:
  8-inch   750 mL
  9-inch   1 litre

Tube pans:
  8x3-inch   2 litre
  9x4-inch   3 litre

Loaf pans:
  8x4x3-inch   1.5 litre
  9x5x3-inch   2 litre

Approximate Equivalent Weights

Apples	1 pound	3 cups sliced or 3 medium-sized
Beans	1 cup (dry)	2½ cups cooked
Bananas	1 pound	1 cup mashed or 3 medium
Bread	1 pound	4 cups
Bread crumbs	1 slice	⅔ cup
Butter:	1 square	½ cup
	1 pound	2 cups
Cheese, grated	1 pound	4 cups
Cherries, glaced (halves)	8 ounces	1 cup
Chocolate	1 ounce	1 square
Cocoa	1 pound	5 cups
Coconut	1 pound	6 cups
Cornmeal	1 pound	3 cups
Cornstarch	1 pound	3½ cups
Crackers:	1 cup	12 graham wafers
	1 cup	18 soda crackers
Cream (whipping)	1 cup	2 cups (whipped)
Currants	1 pound	3 cups
Dates (pitted, chopped)	1 pound	2½ cups
Flour: all-purpose (sifted)	1 pound	4 cups
graham	1 pound	4⅓ cups
rye	1 pound	4¼ cups

whole wheat	1 pound	4¼ cups
self-rising	1 pound	4 cups
Gelatine	¼ ounce	1 envelope or 1 tbsp
Lard	1 pound	2⅓ cups
Lemon	1	2 tbsp grated rind
		3 tbsp juice
Macaroni, spaghetti	1 cup dry	2 cups cooked
Marshmallows	½ pound	32 large marshmallows
		or 5 cups miniature
Noodles	1 pound	7½ cups

(*Noodles do not increase any amount in size when cooked)

Nuts, shelled:

almonds	1 pound	3 cups
peanuts	1 pound	3½ cups
pecan halves	1 pound	4 cups
walnut halves	1 pound	4¼ cups
Onion	1 medium	½ cup, chopped
Orange	1 medium	⅓ cup juice
		2¼ tbsp grated rind
Potatoes	1 pound	2 large potatoes
		3 medium potatoes
		4 small potatoes
		2¼ cups peeled, diced
		2½ cups peeled, sliced
		2 cups mashed
	2 medium	1 cup mashed
		1½ cup diced
		1¾ cups thinly sliced
	1 medium	⅓ pound (5 to 6 ounces)
Raisins: seeded	1 pound	3 cups
seedless	1 pound	2½ cups
Rhubarb	1 pound	2 cups chopped
Rice	1 cup, raw	3 cups, cooked
	1 pound	2¼ cups
Rolled oats	1 pound	6 cups
Shortening	1 pound	2½ cups
Strawberries	1 quart	3½ cups
Suet	½ pound	1½ cups chopped
Sugar: brown	1 pound	2½ cups lightly packed
granulated (white)	1 pound	2¼ cups
icing sugar	1 pound	4 cups sifted
Tomatoes	1 pound	3 medium
		4 small

Common Cooking Terms

á la king	= served in a rich cream sauce containing mushrooms and paprika.
au gratin	= baked or broiled with a bread crumb and/or cheese topping.
bake	= to cook by dry heat in an oven or oven type appliance
barbecue	= to roast meat on a rack or spit, basting with a seasoned sauce.
baste	= pouring liquid or melted fat over food to prevent drying and to add flavour.
batter	= mixture of liquid, flour and other ingredients in thickness ranging from pouring to spreading.
beat	= to incorporate air into a smooth mixture using a brisk over and over motion with a spoon or electric mixer.
blanch	= to loosen skins on fruits and nuts by covering in boiling water then immersing in cold water.
blend	= to thoroughly combine two or more ingredients.
boil	= to heat a liquid until bubbles continually break on the surface.
braise	= to cook slowly in a small amount of liquid in a covered dish.
bread	= to coat with fine bread or cracker crumbs before baking or frying.
broil	= to cook meat by searing the surface on a broiler or over hot coals.
caramelize	= to melt sugar slowly over low heat until it becomes a golden brown syrup.
chop	= to cut food in small pieces with a knife.
clarify	= to make a liquid clear by skimming and filtering out impurities.
coat	= to cover food evenly with flour, crumbs or batter.
coddle	= to cook food slowly in water heated to just below the boiling point.
compote	= fruit cooked in syrup and served as a dessert.
cool	= let food stand at room temperature until no longer warm to the touch.
cream	= to soften fat, such as butter, with a spoon or mixer, until light and fluffy.
cube	= to cut a solid food into cubes about ½ inch or more in size.
cut in	= to combine solid fat with dry ingredients using two knives or a pastry blender.
dice	= to cut into small cubes of ⅛ to ¼ inch with a sharp knife on a cutting board.
dough	= a mixture of flour, liquid and other ingredients thick enough to knead, pat or roll out.
drain	= to remove liquid from a food by placing it in a colander or using a lid.
dredge	= to coat food with a fine dry substance such as flour.

dust	= to sprinkle lightly with sugar or flour.
fillet	= a piece of meat, fish or poultry without bone.
flake	= to break into small pieces, usually with a fork.
flour	= to coat with flour.
flute	= to make a decorative edging around a pie before baking.
fold in	= to combine ingredients without releasing air bubbles. Using a spoon, go down through the mixture on the far side of the bowl, bring the spoon across the bottom of the bowl and up the near side. Give the bowl a quarter turn with each motion.
fricassée	= food that is browned then simmered or baked in a sauce with vegetables.
fry	= to cook in hot fat. Pan fry = cook in a small amount of fat in a frying pan. Deep fry = cook in fat deep enough to cover the food.
garnish	= to decorate with colourful contrasting food.
glacé	= food coated with a sugar syrup.
glaze	= to add lustre to a food by coating with a smooth mixture.
grate	= to shred food by rubbing it against a grater.
grill	= to broil or cook on a rack over hot coals.
grind	= to cut or crush in a grinder, blender or food processor.
julienne	= to cut in matchlike strips.
knead	= to work dough by pressing with the heel of the hand, folding and stretching. Rotate the dough one-quarter of a turn with each press.
marinade	= a mixture of liquid and seasonings used to tenderize food.
marinate	= to let food stand in a seasoned marinade to tenderize.
melt	= to slowly heat a solid substance until it liquefies.
mince	= to grind, chop or cut into very fine pieces.
mix	= to combine ingredients until evenly distributed.
parbroil	= to cook uncovered in a frying pan, draining off fat as it accumulates.
pan boil	= to partly cook in boiling liquid. Then complete the cooking by another method.
pare	= to peel off outer skin.
peel	= to strip off or pull away outer covering of fruit or vegetables.
poach	= to cook slowly in simmering liquid.
pot roast	= a method of cooking cheaper, less tender cuts of meat by browning the surface in fat and then cooking slowly in a small amount of liquid, on top of the stove or in an oven.

purée	= to press cooked food through a fine sieve or to mix in a blender.
reduce	= to simmer a liquid, uncovered, until some of it evaporates.
roast	= to cook meat, uncovered, by dry heat in an oven.
sauté	= to brown or cook in small amount of fat.
scald	= to heat milk until bubbles form around the edge of the dish or to dip food briefly in boiling water.
scallop	= to bake small pieces of food, usually with a cream sauce, in a casserole.
score	= to make criss-cross cuts over the surface of a food with a knife.
sear	= to cook meat at a very high temperature for a short time, to quickly form a crust on the outer surface.
shred	= to cut in long thin strips with a knife or shredder.
simmer	= to cook in liquid, just below the boiling point.
sliver	= to cut into long thin pieces with a knife.
steam	= to cook covered over a small amount of boiling water, so that steam circulates freely around the food.
steep	= to let food soak in liquid until liquid absorbs the food's flavour.
stew	= to cook covered in boiling water.
stir	= to mix together with a spoon using a circular motion.
stir-fry	= to fry, stirring constantly.
toast	= to brown with dry heat in an oven or toaster.
whip	= to beat rapidly with a whisk, beater or mixer to incorporate air. This lightens and increases volume.

Index